FOUN?????   EU

Robert Ba?????   ?Jones

QUINTUS HORATIUS FLACCUS was born in 65 B.C. in Venusia, the Hellenized south-eastern region of Italy. His father was an ex-slave but managed to provide his son with an education under Orbilius in Rome and afterwards sent him to Athens to study philosophy. While in Greece he joined, as an officer, the republican army of Brutus and Cassius and attended the battle of Philippi (42 B.C.) where they were defeated by Octavian (later Augustus) and Anthony. Horace returned to Italy to find his father dead and the family property confiscated. It was during the ensuing years of poverty that he began to write whilst endeavouring to improve his circumstances. Octavian decreed a general amnesty in 39 B.C. which enabled Horace to obtain a minor clerical post in the Treasury, and a year later Virgil introduced him to Maecenas (Octavian's right-hand man in civil affairs). A deep and lasting attachment sprang up between the two men, Maecenas giving to Horace in 34 B.C. a small estate which guaranteed him some peace and security. In 23 B.C. he published the first three books of the *Odes* in the form of eighty-eight *carmina* or songs; but they were not enthusiastically received. He then published in 20 B.C. and 12 B.C.(?) the two books of *Epistles* written in hexameter form. However he composed more odes at the request of Augustus in 17 B.C. and published probably in 13 B.C. his fourth and shortest book of *Odes*. Maecenas died in 8 B.C., recommending Horace to Augustus, but Horace also died within a few weeks of him, naming Augustus as his heir.

JAMES MICHIE was born in 1927 and educated at Marlborough and Trinity College, Oxford, where he read Classics. He is at present a director of the Bodley Head. His publications include *Possible Laughter*.

THE
ODES
OF
HORACE

TRANSLATED
WITH AN INTRODUCTION
BY JAMES MICHIE

4961

PENGUIN BOOKS

Penguin Books Ltd, Harmondsworth,
Middlesex, England
Penguin Books Australia Ltd, Ringwood,
Victoria, Australia

—

This translation first published by Rupert Hart-Davis, 1964
Published in Penguin Books 1967
Reprinted 1970, 1973

—

Copyright © James Michie, 1964

—

Made and printed in Great Britain by
Hazell Watson & Viney Ltd, Aylesbury, Bucks
Set in Monotype Scotch Roman

To my brother Donald

CONTENTS

Translator's Preface   9

Horace: The Man   11

Book One   16

Book Two   90

Book Three   136

Book Four   210

The Centennial Hymn   256

Notes   263

Glossary   276

TRANSLATOR'S PREFACE

Robert Frost once defined poetry as 'what gets lost in translation'. I acknowledge this unpleasant truth. All translation is a form of betrayal, and poetry such as Horace's which is strongly marked by formal qualities suffers most from the treason of clerks. Beyond this point I do not feel like apologising. In these days translation can be a precious lesser evil. It is better that Horace should be 'done down' into English than that he should be undone by the gradual disappearance of Latin as part of our culture. Reinterpreting the Odes, once a dons' parlour game, had become, as I saw it, an urgent rescue operation.

My second, and happier, acknowledgment is to two previous translators, Lord Lytton and Mr J. B. Leishman. Almost a hundred years ago the former devised two felicitous 'equivalents' of the Sapphic and Alcaic metres, and these I have frequently copied or adapted – Book One: XII and XXXV, for example; while the latter's translation of thirty of the Odes into their original metres in 1951 was a courageous and valuable experiment – particularly valuable from my point of view because I think that it unwittingly demonstrated that Alcaics could be strictly and successfully naturalised, but that the same did not apply to Sapphics. Persuaded by Mr Leishman, I have put the following thirteen Odes (eleven of them Alcaic) into the original metres: Book One: IV, V, IX, XXVII, XXXI; Book Two: III, XIV, XV; Book Three: XVII, XXI, XXIII; Book Four: VII, XV. Horace adopted Alcaics in thirty-seven and Sapphics in twenty-six of his 104 Odes (including the Carmen Saeculare), and diversified the rest by the use of more than a dozen other metres. I have done my best to reflect this virtuoso variety. Where my own metre may be thought incongruous (Book Four: IX ?) I plead that it was not chosen in accordance with some preconceived theory but seemed to choose itself after more obvious approaches had failed. Lack of time and industry have prevented me from including the early, and underestimated, Epodes, and for this only half-deliberate omission I am sorry.

I have used the Latin text of the Oxford University Press edition, which is reproduced except for the substitution of a few variant readings or emendations which I have preferred. These preferences are: Book One: IV, 8, 'urit'; VIII, 2, 'te deos oro'; XII, 31, 'quod'; XII, 46, 'Marcellis'; XV, 20, 'crines'; XXV, 20, 'Euro'. Book Three: III, 12, 'bibet'; III, 34, 'discere'; IV, 9, 'avio'; V, 15, 'trahenti'; XIV, 11, 'non'; XXIV, 4, 'publicum'. Book Four: II, 49, 'tuque'; XIV, 20, 'indomitus'. Carmen Saeculare: 68–72, 'proroget . . . curet . . . applicet'. In four places I have preferred a punctuation favoured by other editors: Book One: XII, 20; Book Two: X, 6; Book Three: XXIII, 17–18 and XXIV, 41–4.

I am especially grateful to Mr Rex Warner for his encouragement, given when I needed it most, at the beginning, before momentum had overcome despair. I should also like to thank my publishers, Mr Rupert Hart-Davis and Mr Howard Greenfield of the Orion Press, for their patience, promptness and generosity; Mr Nicolas Barker for his courteous help; and Mr John Coates for assembling the Notes and Glossary.

J. M.

HORACE: THE MAN

Quintus Horatius Flaccus was born in B.C. 65 in Venusia, a small town in the Hellenised south-eastern region of Italy. His father was an ex-slave who had gained his freedom, possibly for services to the municipality, obtained a job as tax-collector or auctioneer's assistant (*coactor*) and settled down in possession of a little land. Of his mother nothing is known. The elder Horace, whom his son called 'the best of fathers', was clearly a remarkable man. He managed to provide his boy with an education under the eminent teacher Orbilius in Rome and afterwards sent him to Athens to study philosophy. There Horace must have learned the news of Julius Caesar's assassination; soon afterwards Marcus Brutus passed through the city on his way to take up the pro-praetorship of Macedonia, and when Brutus and Cassius later raised an army to oppose Octavian and Antony, Horace, together with his idealistic fellow students, rallied to the cause of 'freedom'. As an officer he attended the battle of Philippi (B.C. 42), where republican hopes were crushed, and escaped, 'leaving my poor shield disgracefully behind', as he self-deprecatingly puts it. At the age of twenty-three he returned to Italy to find his father dead and his family property confiscated.

According to Horace, poverty drove him to try his hand at verses, but we need not take this any more seriously than Dr. Johnson's assertion that 'no man but a blockhead ever wrote except for money'. During the next ten years he occupied himself with the composition of the seventeen Epodes – caustic iambic poems in the manner of Archilochus, the seventh-century poet of Paros – and the two books of Satires in hexameters, and his circumstances steadily improved. In B.C. 39 Octavian decreed a general amnesty, which enabled him to get himself a minor clerical post in the Treasury, and in the following year Virgil, who had come to know and admire the younger poet, introduced him to Maecenas, Octavian's right-hand man in civil affairs. A deep and lasting attachment sprang up between the two men. In B.C. 37 Horace accompanied Maecenas on an important mission to Brundisium, and about B.C. 34 Maecenas made his friend the gift of the famous Sabine farm, which lay ten miles north-east of Tibur (the modern Tivoli). To be precise, it was a small estate run by a foreman and eight slaves ('boys'), with five tenant farms attached. At one stroke Horace was presented with security, an escape from the noise and nastiness of the capital and a chance to enjoy the pleasures of the countryside and to play the host in a modest way; and so tactful was the patron that the beneficiary seems to have felt no loss of independence. We know that Horace also spent a great deal of time at Tibur, though it is uncertain whether he had a house there, as was believed in Suetonius' time, or merely stayed with friends.

Since the treaty of Brundisium (B.C. 40), by which Italy and the western provinces were assigned to Octavian and the whole of the East to Antony, Octavian's intelligent attempts at agricultural reform and his propaganda campaign to revive the ancient Roman austerities had made themselves felt and the country was beginning to enjoy some measure of stability. When the split between Octavian and Antony became irreparable, the former was able successfully to call upon the patriotism of the Italians to 'defend themselves' in an aggressive war against 'the effeminate East', and after the sea-battle of Actium (B.C. 31), at which Antony was left helpless by the defection of Cleopatra's fleet, Rome was free to turn her energies to imperial expansion. In B.C. 27 Octavian arranged for the Senate to confer on him the title of Augustus* ('Worshipful') and did not discourage the populace from honouring him as a demigod (see Book Four, Ode V). The autocracy was, for good or bad, firmly established.

In B.C. 23 Horace published the fruit of a decade's work, the first three books of the Odes – eighty-eight *carmina*, or songs, remarkable, apart from their other qualities, for the skill with which a variety of Greek metres were adapted to suit the more lapidary character of the Latin language. Unlike Virgil's

* In translating the Odes I have called Octavian 'Augustus' regardless of strict chronology.

Aeneid, which appeared four years later, the Odes did not win the widespread appreciation that Horace may have expected. Perhaps this was the reason why he seems to have temporarily abandoned ode-writing and returned to the hexameter form, in which he cast his two books of Epistles, elegant and witty reflections on literature and morality, published in B.C. 20 and 12? respectively. Whatever caused this lyrical silence, it was broken in B.C. 17, when Augustus, in accordance with his policy of reviving ancient Roman customs, decided to stage the long-discontinued Secular Games as an international showpiece and commanded Horace to compose the *Carmen Saeculare,* an ode to be sung in the temple of Apollo by a choir of boys and girls. Soon afterwards the Emperor commissioned him to write odes on the victories of his stepsons, Drusus and Tiberius. Either creatively stimulated by this official compliment, or drawing on what he had meanwhile written but not published, in B.C. 13 or later Horace gave the public his fourth and shortest book of Odes. The next five years are unrecorded. In B.C. 8 Maecenas died, requesting Augustus to 'remember Horatius Flaccus as you will remember me'. The Emperor, who had at one time invited the poet to be his private secretary only to have the offer politely declined, did not have much time in which to express his esteem. Within a few weeks, in his fifty-seventh year, Horace was also dead, so fulfilling the prophecy in Book Two, Ode XVII. He named Augustus as his heir.

At forty-four Horace described himself as 'of small stature, fond of the sun, prematurely grey, quick-tempered but easily placated'. We are lucky to have even that glimpse of him, for the writers of the Ancient World were not inclined to self-portraits. In the Odes Greek sophistication and melancholy alternate with Italian vigour and rhetoric, and behind both there lurks a personal irony, the intensity of which it is hard in places to gauge. Sometimes it irradiates a whole poem, sometimes it gleams dubiously in a word. One has the impression of a strong but elusive personality, one whose solidity is enhanced rather than diminished by surface inconsistencies, a temperament with a capacity for digesting the hard tack of life. How deep were his religious feelings? How whole-heartedly did he support the regime? It is unwise to argue about the exact degree of heat of his intellectual allegiances. Like many educated Romans Horace probably believed in the traditional pantheon for social purposes. Had not Julius Caesar, a known sceptic, bribed his way to the highest ecclesiastical post, that of Pontifex Maximus? Like touching wood, reference to the gods was a reflex instinct; in the Epicurean philosophy the gods were not abolished but placed outside the world and its concerns. At all events religious belief was poetically, if not intellectually, alive enough in sophisticated Rome for the Bacchus, Mercury, Diana and Faunus of the Odes to be more than painted-on figures, to glow as numinous presences. As for Horace's political convictions, it is hard to believe that he nourished any secret nostalgia for the Republic. No doubt he disapproved of some of Augustus's measures: we cannot know. But if the Emperor expected a tame poet to undertake the full duties of laureateship, he met a master of the graceful sidestep, as 1, VI and 2, XII demonstrate. Few of the Odes are directly political and exhortatory, and even some of these are not rigorously straight-faced. Imagine Tennyson's 'Ode on the Death of the Duke of Wellington' ending with a verse as cavalier as the last one in 2, I! Many of them are addressed to friends or lovers – of either sex. Even when they appear to deal with public affairs, they often succeed only in suggesting the importance of private life. If they are in Gilbert Highet's words 'one of the few absolutely central and unchallengeable classics in Latin and the whole of western literature', it is not because of their decorative or escapist qualities, but because in them love and friendship and civilised enjoyment are balanced against death and bloodshed and the duties that belong to civilisation: the scales tremble, but the poet's hand is steady: it is the exciting equilibrium of mature art.

J. M.

Q

HORATI

FLACCI

CARMINUM

LIBER PRIMUS

THE ODES OF

HORACE

BOOK

ONE

I

Maecenas atavis edite regibus,
o et praesidium et dulce decus meum,
sunt quos curriculo pulverem Olympicum
collegisse iuvat, metaque fervidis
evitata rotis palmaque nobilis
terrarum dominos evehit ad deos;
hunc, si mobilium turba Quiritium
certat tergeminis tollere honoribus;
illum, si proprio condidit horreo
quidquid de Libycis verritur areis.
gaudentem patrios findere sarculo
agros Attalicis condicionibus
numquam dimoveas ut trabe Cypria
Myrtoum pavidus nauta secet mare.
luctantem Icariis fluctibus Africum
mercator metuens otium et oppidi
laudat rura sui; mox reficit ratis
quassas, indocilis pauperiem pati.
est qui nec veteris pocula Massici
nec partem solido demere de die
spernit, nunc viridi membra sub arbuto
stratus, nunc ad aquae lene caput sacrae.
multos castra iuvant et lituo tubae
permixtus sonitus bellaque matribus
detestata. manet sub Iove frigido
venator tenerae coniugis immemor,
seu visa est catulis cerva fidelibus,
seu rupit teretes Marsus aper plagas.
me doctarum hederae praemia frontium
dis miscent superis, me gelidum nemus
nympharumque leves cum Satyris chori
secernunt populo, si neque tibias
Euterpe cohibet nec Polyhymnia
Lesboum refugit tendere barbiton.

1

Maecenas, son of royal stock,
My friend, my honour, my firm rock,
The enthusiastic charioteer
Stirs up the Olympic dust, then, clear-
ing turning-post with red-hot wheels,
Snatches the victor's palm and feels
Lord of the earth, god among men;
The politician glories when
The fickle voters designate
Him three times public magistrate;
A third if in his barns he stores
All Libya's wheat-stacked threshing floors.
The peasant happy with a rake
Scratching his family fields won't take
Even an Attaline reward
To face the terrors of shipboard,
An awkward landsman trying to plough
Salt furrows with a Cyprian prow.
The trader, when the southerly gales
Tussle the waves round Samos, quails
And grumbles for a life of ease,
For his home town and fields and trees,
But, ill-disposed to learn to be
A poor man, soon refits for sea
His tossed ships. One man won't decline
Goblets of vintage Massic wine,
Or stolen time, a solid chunk
Of afternoon, sprawled by the trunk
Of a green arbutus, or spread-
eagled by some quiet fountain-head.
Another likes the life at arms,
The camp's cacophonous alarms –
Bugle and clarion – and the wars
Mothers abominate. Outdoors,

quodsi me lyricis vatibus inseres,
sublimi feriam sidera vertice.

II

Iam satis terris nivis atque dirae
grandinis misit Pater et rubente
dextera sacras iaculatus arces
    terruit urbem,

terruit gentis, grave ne rediret
saeculum Pyrrhae nova monstra questae,
omne cum Proteus pecus egit altos
    visere montis,

piscium et summa genus haesit ulmo
nota quae sedes fuerat columbis,
et superiecto pavidae natarunt
    aequore dammae.

Underneath the freezing skies,
Contentedly the hunter lies,
Oblivious of his sweet young bride
When once his trusty dogs have spied
Deer, or a Marsian wild boar tears
The fine-spun netting of his snares.
But me the crown of ivy, sign
Of poets' brows, denotes divine;
Me the light troop, in the cool glen,
Of nymphs and satyrs screens from men –
While Euterpe still lets me use
Her twin pipes, and her sister Muse
Consents to tune the Lesbian lyre.
And if to the great lyric choir
You add my name, this head, held high,
Will jog the planets in the sky.

2

Enough the ordeal now, the snow- and hail-storms
God has unleashed on earth, whose red right hand hurled
Bolts at the Capitol's sacred summits, spreading
　　Fear in the City streets,

Fear among nations lest the age of horror
Should come again when Pyrrha gasped at strange sights:
Old Proteus herding his whole sea-zoo uphill,
　　Visiting mountain-tops,

And the fish people, tangled in the elm-trees,
Floundering among the ancient haunts of pigeons,
And deer in terror struggling through the new-spread
　　Fields of a world-wide flood.

vidimus flavum Tiberim retortis
litore Etrusco violenter undis
ire deiectum monumenta regis
    templaque Vestae,

Iliae dum se nimium querenti
iactat ultorem, vagus et sinistra
labitur ripa Iove non probante u-
    xorius amnis.

audiet civis acuisse ferrum
quo graves Persae melius perirent,
audiet pugnas vitio parentum
    rara iuventus.

quem vocet divum populus ruentis
imperi rebus? prece qua fatigent
virgines sanctae minus audientem
    carmina Vestam?

cui dabit partis scelus expiandi
Iuppiter? tandem venias precamur
nube candentis umeros amictus,
    augur Apollo;

sive tu mavis, Erycina ridens,
quam Iocus circum volat et Cupido;
sive neglectum genus et nepotes
    respicis auctor,

heu nimis longo satiate ludo,
quem iuvat clamor galeaeque leves
acer et Mauri peditis cruentum
    vultus in hostem;

sive mutata iuvenem figura
ales in terris imitaris almae

We watched the Tiber's tawny water, wrenched back
Hard from the Tuscan side, go raging forward
To Vesta's temple and King Numa's palace,
   Threatening their overthrow.

Wild, love-lorn river god! He saw himself as
Avenger of his long-lamenting Ilia
And trespassed left across his banks, thus crossing
   Jupiter's wishes too.

The old have sinned; survivors of their errors,
Thinned ranks, the young shall hear how brothers sharpened
Against each other swords that should have carried
   Death to the Parthian pest.

Which of the gods now shall the people summon
To prop Rome's reeling sovereignty? What prayer
Shall the twelve Virgins use to reach the ear of
   Vesta, who grows each day

Deafer to litanies? Whom shall the Father
Appoint as instrument of our atonement?
Come, augur god, Apollo, come, we pray thee,
   Glittering shoulders hid

In cloud; or thou, gay goddess of Mount Eryx,
Desire and Laughter fluttering in attendance;
Or thou, great parent of our race, grown tired of
   Relishing war, that long,

Sad game, the battle-cries, the flashing helmets,
The bloodsoaked legionary, the Moor's ferocious
Glare as they meet – O Mars, if still regarding
   Us, thy neglected sons,

Come; or else thou, winged boy of gentle Maia,
Put on the mortal shape of a young Roman,

filius Maiae patiens vocari
 Caesaris ultor:

serus in caelum redeas diuque
laetus intersis populo Quirini,
neve te nostris vitiis iniquum
 ocior aura

tollat; hic magnos potius triumphos,
hic ames dici pater atque princeps,
neu sinas Medos equitare inultos
 te duce, Caesar.

III

Sic te diva potens Cypri,
sic fratres Helenae, lucida sidera,
 ventorumque regat pater
obstrictis aliis praeter Iapyga,
 navis, quae tibi creditum
debes Vergilium, finibus Atticis
 reddas incolumem precor,
et serves animae dimidium meae.
 illi robur et aes triplex
circa pectus erat, qui fragilem truci
 commisit pelago ratem
primus, nec timuit praecipitem Africum
 decertantem Aquilonibus
nec tristis Hyadas nec rabiem Noti,
 quo non arbiter Hadriae
maior, tollere seu ponere vult freta.
 quem mortis timuit gradum,
qui siccis oculis monstra natantia,
 qui vidit mare turbidum et
infamis scopulos Acroceraunia?

Descend and, well contented to be known as
  Caesar's avenger, stay

Gladly and long with Romulus's people,
Delaying late thy homeward, skybound journey,
And may no whirlwind prematurely snatch thee,
  Wrath with our sins, away.

Rather on earth enjoy resplendent triumphs;
Be Prince, be Father – titles to rejoice in;
And let no Parthian raider ride unscathed while
  Caesar has charge of Rome.

3

Fare forward, good ship, and, I pray,
May Venus, queen of Cyprus, may
Helen's bright brothers, masthead stars,
And may (all winds kept behind bars
But the north-west) the god of gales
Aeolus so direct your sails
That you who voyage promise-bound
To keep your cargo safe and sound
Deliver to his Attic goal
Virgil, and with him half my soul.
Whoever first presumed to float
On the grim sea a brittle boat
Must have had ribs of oak and three
Integuments of brass to be
Undaunted by the Hyads' surly
Sign, the ferocious hurly-burly
Of north-east wrestling with south-west,
And the wild south wind, powerfullest
Lord in the Adriatic quarter
To ruffle or make smooth the water.

nequiquam deus abscidit
prudens Oceano dissociabili
terras, si tamen impiae
non tangenda rates transiliunt vada.
audax omnia perpeti
gens humana ruit per vetitum nefas.
audax Iapeti genus
ignem fraude mala gentibus intulit.
post ignem aetheria domo
subductum macies et nova febrium
terris incubuit cohors,
semotique prius tarda necessitas
leti corripuit gradum.
expertus vacuum Daedalus aera
pennis non homini datis:
perrupit Acheronta Herculeus labor.
nil mortalibus ardui est:
caelum ipsum petimus stultitia neque
per nostrum patimur scelus
iracunda Iovem ponere fulmina.

IV

Solvitur acris hiems grata vice veris et Favoni,
trahuntque siccas machinae carinas,
ac neque iam stabulis gaudet pecus aut arator igni,
nec prata canis albicant pruinis.

Could death's close footstep unnerve him
Who, dry-eyed, watched sea-monsters swim
In the wild surge, and the cliffs loom
Up from Epirus, coast of doom?
In vain God in his wisdom planned
The ocean separate from the land
If ships, defying his intent,
Cross the forbidden element.
Man dares and bears all, rushing in
To trespass upon every sin.
Prometheus dared in fetching men
Fire by a wicked theft, yet when
The flame was filched from heaven's courts
Wasting diseases, fresh cohorts
Of fevers fell on land and sea,
And leisurely mortality
Leapt with accelerated pace.
Daedalus challenging empty space
With home-made wings was one of these
Adventurers; so was Hercules
The Labourer, who burst Hell's portals.
No barrier is too high for mortals:
In our foolhardiness we try
To escalade the very sky.
Still we presumptuously aspire,
And still with unabated ire
Jove hurls his thunderbolts of fire.

4

Winter relaxes its grip. West winds are a pleasant change.
    The spring's here.
  The windlasses haul down the dry hulls seaward;
Penned in the stable, the beasts grow fretful; the farmer
    loves his fire less;
  The fields no longer shine with morning whiteness.

iam Cytherea choros ducit Venus imminente Luna,
    iunctaeque Nymphis Gratiae decentes
alterno terram quatiunt pede, dum gravis Cyclopum
    Vulcanus ardens urit officinas.
nunc decet aut viridi nitidum caput impedire myrto
    aut flore terrae quem ferunt solutae;
nunc et in umbrosis Fauno decet immolare lucis,
    seu poscat agna sive malit haedo.
pallida Mors aequo pulsat pede pauperum tabernas
    regumque turris. o beate Sesti,
vitae summa brevis spem nos vetat incohare longam.
    iam te premet nox fabulaeque Manes
et domus exilis Plutonia; quo simul mearis,
    nec regna vini sortiere talis,
nec tenerum Lycidan mirabere, quo calet iuventus
    nunc omnis et mox virgines tepebunt.

V

Quis multa gracilis te puer in rosa
perfusus liquidis urget odoribus
    grato, Pyrrha, sub antro ?
      cui flavam religas comam,

simplex munditiis ? heu quotiens fidem
mutatosque deos flebit et aspera
    nigris aequora ventis
      emirabitur insolens,

Queening the dance, with a full moon hanging above, the
   Cytherean
  Leads, and the Nymphs and comely Graces follow,
Stamping the ground to the beat, hands linked. In the
   Cyclops' sweltering workshop
  Red-visaged Vulcan sets the forges blazing.
Now heads glossy with oil sport wreaths of the season's vivid
   myrtle
  Or the few blooms unclenching earth releases.
Time, too, now in the leaf-dark groves for a sacrifice to
   Faunus –
  A lamb, or else a kid, if he prefers it.
Hold! Pale Death, at the poor man's shack and the pasha's
   palace kicking
  Impartially, announces his arrival.
Life's brief tenure forbids high hopes to be built in
   disproportion,
  My lucky Sestius, for Night and Pluto's
Shadowy walls and the ghosts men talk of will soon be
   crowding round you.
  Once there, you cannot rule the feast by dice-throw
Or give Lycidas long rapt gazes. This year his beauty kindles
  The young men: soon the girls will catch fire also.

5

What slim youngster, his hair dripping with fragrant oil,
Makes hot love to you now, Pyrrha, ensconced in a
  Snug cave curtained with roses?
    Who lays claim to that casually

Chic blonde hair in a braid? Soon he'll be scolding the
Gods, whose promise, like yours, failed him, and gaping at
  Black winds making his ocean's
    Fair face unrecognisable.

qui nunc te fruitur credulus aurea,
qui semper vacuam, semper amabilem
   sperat, nescius aurae
     fallacis! miseri, quibus

intemptata nites. me tabula sacer
votiva paries indicat uvida
   suspendisse potenti
     vestimenta maris deo.

VI

Scriberis Vario fortis et hostium
victor Maeonii carminis alite,
quam rem cumque ferox navibus aut equis
   miles te duce gesserit:

nos, Agrippa, neque haec dicere nec gravem
Pelidae stomachum cedere nescii
nec cursus duplicis per mare Ulixei
   nec saevam Pelopis domum

conamur, tenues grandia, dum pudor
imbellisque lyrae Musa potens vetat
laudes egregii Caesaris et tuas
   culpa deterere ingeni.

He's still credulous, though, hugging the prize he thinks
Pure gold, shining and fond, his for eternity.
  Ah, poor fool, but the breeze plays
    Tricks.   Doomed, all who would venture to

Sail that glittering sea. Fixed to the temple wall,
My plaque tells of an old sailor who foundered and,
  Half-drowned, hung up his clothes to
    Neptune, lord of the element.

6

    That eagle of Homeric wing
      Varius will in due course sing
    Your courage and your conquests, every deed
      Of daring that our forces,
      Riding on ships or horses,
    Accomplish with Agrippa in the lead.

    But I'm not strong enough to try
      Such epic flights. For themes as high
    As iron Achilles in his savage pique,
      Crafty Ulysses homing
      After long ocean-roaming,
    Or Pelops' house of blood, my wings feel weak;

    And both my modesty and my Muse,
      Who tunes her lyre to peace, refuse
    To let me tarnish in the laureate's part
      Our glorious Augustus'
      Or your own battle-lustres
    With my imperfect and unpolished art.

quis Martem tunica tectum adamantina
digne scripserit aut pulvere Troico
nigrum Merionen aut ope Palladis
    Tydiden superis parem?

nos convivia, nos proelia virginum
sectis in iuvenes unguibus acrium
cantamus vacui, sive quid urimur
    non praeter solitum leves.

VII

Laudabunt alii claram Rhodon aut Mytilenen
    aut Epheson bimarisve Corinthi
moenia vel Baccho Thebas vel Apolline Delphos
    insignis aut Thessala Tempe:
sunt quibus unum opus est intactae Palladis urbem
    carmine perpetuo celebrare et
undique decerptam fronti praeponere olivam:
    plurimus in Iunonis honorem
aptum dicet equis Argos ditisque Mycenas:
    me nec tam patiens Lacedaemon
nec tam Larisae percussit campus opimae,
    quam domus Albuneae resonantis
et praeceps Anio ac Tiburni lucus et uda
    mobilibus pomaria rivis.
albus ut obscuro deterget nubila caelo
    saepe Notus neque parturit imbris
perpetuo, sic tu sapiens finire memento
    tristitiam vitaeque labores
molli, Plance, mero, seu te fulgentia signis
    castra tenent seu densa tenebit

Can any poet recreate
A worthy portrait of the great
Meriones blackened with Trojan dirt,
Or Diomede attacking
Gods with Athene's backing,
Or Mars dressed in his adamantine shirt?

Feasts, and the wars where girls' trimmed nails
Scratch fiercely at besieging males –
These are the subjects that appeal to me,
Flippant, as is my fashion,
Whether the flame of passion
Has scorched me or has left me fancy-free.

7

Others can praise in their verse Mitylene, Rhodes and its
    glories,
    Great Ephesus, high-walled, twin-harboured Corinth,
Bacchus's home town Thebes, or Delphi, haunt of Apollo,
    Or Tempe up in Thessaly. Some poets
Concentrate all their lives on a long-drawn epic extolling
    Virgin Athene's city, plucking sprigs of
Olive from Attica's history, wreaths to adorn their foreheads;
    And some, to honour Juno's reputation,
Celebrate Argos, country for horses, and rich Mycenae.
    But, as for me, neither the sturdy Spartan
Hills nor the low lush fields of Larissa can knock at the
    heart as
    My Tibur does, the Sibyl's booming grotto,
Anio's fine cascade, Tiburnus' grove and the orchards
    Whose rivulets weave a dance of irrigation.
Winds from the south blow clear; they sweep clouds out of a
    dark sky
    And never breed long rains: remember, Plancus,

Tiburis umbra tui. Teucer Salamina patremque
    cum fugeret, tamen uda Lyaeo
tempora populea fertur vinxisse corona,
    sic tristis adfatus amicos:
'quo nos cumque feret melior fortuna parente,
    ibimus, o socii comitesque.
nil desperandum Teucro duce et auspice: Teucri
    certus enim promisit Apollo
ambiguam tellure nova Salamina futuram.
    o fortes peioraque passi
mecum saepe viri, nunc vino pellite curas;
    cras ingens iterabimus aequor.'

VIII

    Lydia, dic, per omnis
te deos oro, Sybarin cur properes amando
    perdere, cur apricum
oderit campum, patiens pulveris atque solis,
    cur neque militaris
inter aequalis equitet, Gallica nec lupatis
    temperet ora frenis?
cur timet flavum Tiberim tangere? cur olivum
    sanguine viperino
cautius vitat neque iam livida gestat armis
    bracchia, saepe disco,

Good wine does just that for the wise man – chases away all
    The stresses and distresses of existence.
Hold to this truth in the camp, hemmed round by the
    glittering standards,
    And, when you come home soon to Tibur's leafy
Privacy, keep it in mind. When Teucer was sent into exile
    From Salamis by his father, undismayed he
Set on his wine-flushed brow, they say, brave garlands of
    poplar
    And cried to his dispirited companions:
'Fortune will prove more kind than a parent. Wherever she
    takes us,
    Thither, my friends and comrades, we shall follow.
Teucer shall lead and his star shall preside. No cause for
    despair, then.
    Phoebus, who never lies, has pledged a second
Salamis, rival in name, to arise in a new-found country.
    You who have stayed by me through worse disasters,
Heroes, come, drink deep, let wine extinguish our sorrows.
    We take the huge sea on again tomorrow.'

8

Tell us, Lydia, please,
By all the gods, why are you making him weak at the knees
    With love? Why does he whom sun
Nor dust could ever deter effeminately shun
    The heat-baked exercise-ground?
Why is the Sybaris we once knew no longer found
    Among his fellow cadets
On a horse from Gaul with a wolf's-tooth bit, doing curvets?
    He funks the Tiber in flood,
He's shyer of athlete's oil than if it were adder's blood;
    Last year he used to throw
Discus and javelin record lengths – now can he show
    One weapon-bruise on his arm?

saepe trans finem iaculo nobilis expedito ?
   quid latet, ut marinae
filium dicunt Thetidis sub lacrimosa Troiae
   funera, ne virilis
cultus in caedem et Lycias proriperet catervas ?

IX

Vides ut alta stet nive candidum
Soracte, nec iam sustineant onus
   silvae laborantes, geluque
     flumina constiterint acuto.

dissolve frigus ligna super foco
large reponens atque benignius
   deprome quadrimum Sabina,
     o Thaliarche, merum diota:

permitte divis cetera, qui simul
stravere ventos aequore fervido
   deproeliantis, nec cupressi
     nec veteres agitantur orni.

quid sit futurum cras fuge quaerere et
quem Fors dierum cumque dabit lucro
   appone, nec dulcis amores
     sperne puer neque tu choreas,

donec virenti canities abest
morosa. nunc et campus et areae
   lenesque sub noctem susurri
     composita repetantur hora,

nunc et latentis proditor intimo
gratus puellae risus ab angulo
   pignusque dereptum lacertis
     aut digito male pertinaci.

Why does he skulk like this, out of the way of harm,
    As sea-born Thetis's boy
Achilles did, they say, in the sad twilight of Troy,
    Fearful lest man's attire
Should sweep him into the grave and the Lycian line of fire?

9

Look how the snow lies deeply on glittering
Soracte. White woods groan and protestingly
    Let fall their branch-loads. Bitter frost has
        Paralysed rivers: the ice is solid.

Unfreeze the cold! Pile plenty of logs in the
Fireplace! And you, dear friend Thaliarchus, come,
    Bring out the Sabine wine-jar four years
        Old and be generous. Let the good gods

Take care of all else. Later, as soon as they've
Calmed down this contestation of winds upon
    Churned seas, the old ash-trees can rest in
        Peace and the cypresses stand unshaken.

Try not to guess what lies in the future, but
As Fortune deals days enter them into your
    Life's book as windfalls, credit items,
        Gratefully. Now that you're young, and peevish

Grey hairs are still far distant, attend to the
Dance-floor, the heart's sweet business; for now is the
    Right time for midnight assignations,
        Whispers and murmurs in Rome's piazzas

And fields, and soft, low laughter that gives away
The girl who plays love's games in a hiding-place –
    Off comes a ring coaxed down an arm or
        Pulled from a faintly resisting finger.

X

Mercuri, facunde nepos Atlantis,
qui feros cultus hominum recentum
voce formasti catus et decorae
    more palaestrae,

te canam, magni Iovis et deorum
nuntium curvaeque lyrae parentem,
callidum quidquid placuit iocoso
    condere furto.

te, boves olim nisi reddidisses
per dolum amotas, puerum minaci
voce dum terret, viduus pharetra
    risit Apollo.

quin et Atridas duce te superbos
Ilio dives Priamus relicto
Thessalosque ignis et iniqua Troiae
    castra fefellit.

tu pias laetis animas reponis
sedibus virgaque levem coerces
aurea turbam, superis deorum
    gratus et imis.

10

Great Mercury, by Maia sprung
From Atlas; god of nimble tongue
  And understanding; saviour
Of our raw race, who deigned to teach
Man wrestling, grace of body, speech
  And civilised behaviour,

You are the one my poem sings –
The lyre's inventor; he who brings
  Heaven's messages; the witty
Adventurer who takes delight
In slyly stowing out of sight
  Anything he finds pretty.

We know the tale of vengeance vowed –
How Phoebus stormed, while you looked cowed:
  'The herd must be recovered,
Rogue, that you took from me by guile,
Or else . . .' But the god was forced to smile
  Through rage when he discovered

His quiver too filched by a boy!
Carrying ransom out of Troy,
  Priam by you came guided.
Past enemy tents, past the proud sons
Of Atreus, past the Myrmidons'
  Watch-fires, unseen he glided.

You also, golden staff in hand,
Shepherd the good souls' ghostly band
  To the Elysian bowers,
Great Mercury, accorded love
Equally by the gods above
  And the infernal powers.

XI

Tu ne quaesieris, scire nefas, quem mihi, quem tibi
finem di dederint, Leuconoe, nec Babylonios
temptaris numeros. ut melius, quidquid erit, pati,
seu pluris hiemes seu tribuit Iuppiter ultimam,
quae nunc oppositis debilitat pumicibus mare
Tyrrhenum: sapias, vina liques, et spatio brevi
spem longam reseces. dum loquimur, fugerit invida
aetas: carpe diem, quam minimum credula postero.

XII

Quem virum aut heroa lyra vel acri
tibia sumis celebrare, Clio?
quem deum? cuius recinet iocosa
    nomen imago

aut in umbrosis Heliconis oris
aut super Pindo gelidove in Haemo,
unde vocalem temere insecutae
    Orphea silvae

11

Don't ask (we may not know), Leuconoe,
   What the gods plan for you or me.
      Leave the Chaldees to parse
      The sentence of the stars.

Better to bear the outcome, good or bad,
   Whether Jove purposes to add
      Fresh winters to the past
      Or to make this the last

Which now tires out the Tuscan sea and mocks
   Its strength with barricades of rocks.
      Be wise, strain clear the wine
      And prune the rambling vine

Of expectation. Life's short. Even while
   We talk Time, hateful, runs a mile.
      Don't trust tomorrow's bough
      For fruit. Pluck this, here, now.

12

What man, what hero, Clio, will you single
For celebration on the lyre or clear-voiced
Flute? Or a god is it? Whose name shall Echo
   Play with exuberantly

Over Mount Helicon's umbrageous uplands,
The top of Pindus, or the snow-cool shoulder
Of Haemus where a mob of trees once followed
   Orpheus to hear him sing?

arte materna rapidos morantem
fluminum lapsus celerisque ventos,
blandum et auritas fidibus canoris
    ducere quercus?

quid prius dicam solitis parentis
laudibus, qui res hominum ac deorum,
qui mare et terras variisque mundum
    temperat horis?

unde nil maius generatur ipso,
nec viget quicquam simile aut secundum:
proximos illi tamen occupavit
    Pallas honores,

proeliis audax, neque te silebo,
Liber, et saevis inimica Virgo
beluis, nec te, metuende certa
    Phoeba sagitta.

dicam et Alciden puerosque Ledae,
hunc equis, illum superare pugnis
nobilem; quorum simul alba nautis
    stella refulsit,

defluit saxis agitatus umor,
concidunt venti fugiuntque nubes,
et minax, quod sic voluere, ponto
    unda recumbit.

Romulum post hos prius an quietum
Pompili regnum memorem an superbos
Tarquini fascis, dubito, an Catonis
    nobile letum.

Regulum et Scauros animaeque magnae
prodigum Paulum superante Poeno
gratus insigni referam Camena
    Fabriciumque.

(He by the art the Muse his mother taught him
Could check a raging wind or racing river
And touch the strings so sweetly that the charmed oaks
   Flocked to him, each leaf rapt.)

How but, as custom bids, with Jove the Father's
Praises begin, ruler of gods and mortals,
Who governs with the cycle of the seasons
   Ocean and earth and sky,

Creator greater than all things created,
Unparalleled, immortal, undisputed?
Yet next of place there must be, and that honour
   Pallas Athene holds,

Savage in war. Nor shall I pass thee over,
Bacchus, nor her, sworn harrier of monsters,
The Virgin, nor Apollo, the tremendous
   Archer whose shafts go home.

Here too I shall praise Hercules, and with him
That famous pair, the horseman and the boxer,
Leda's twin sons: when sailors see their star-sign
   Glittering bright and clear,

The wild spray slides obedient from the rock-face,
The gales die down, the clouds make off, the huge wave
Towering above the boat sinks, at their bidding,
   Back to the ocean bed.

Whom shall I name next – Romulus? King Numa
Whose reign brought peace? Proud Tarquin with his fasces?
Or should I rather call to mind the noble
   Fashion of Cato's death?

The Scauri, Regulus, Aemilius Paulus
Who paid his great soul down when Carthage triumphed –
These names I write with gratitude; my native
   Muse shall record their worth,

hunc et incomptis Curium capillis
utilem bello tulit et Camillum
saeva paupertas et avitus apto
    cum lare fundus.

crescit occulto velut arbor aevo
fama Marcellis; micat inter omnis
Iulium sidus velut inter ignis
    luna minores.

gentis humanae pater atque custos,
orte Saturno, tibi cura magni
Caesaris fatis data: tu secundo
    Caesare regnes.

ille seu Parthos Latio imminentis
egerit iusto domitos triumpho,
sive subiectos Orientis orae
    Seras et Indos,

te minor laetum reget aequus orbem;
tu gravi curru quaties Olympum,
tu parum castis inimica mittes
    fulmina lucis.

XIII

    Cum tu, Lydia, Telephi
cervicem roseam, cerea Telephi
    laudas bracchia, vae meum
fervens difficili bile tumet iecur.
    tum nec mens mihi nec color
certa sede manent, umor et in genas

Fabricius too, Camillus and unbarbered
Curius – all men whom hard lives and the yeoman's
Long heritage of farm and family homestead
   Bred to the soldier's mould.

The fame of the Marcelli still increases
By growth invisible, like a tree's; the Julian
Star still ascends, a moon among the lesser
   Fires of the firmament.

Thou son of Saturn, father and protector
Of humankind, to thee Fate has entrusted
Care of great Caesar; govern, then, while Caesar
   Holds the lieutenancy.

He, whether leading in entitled triumph
The Parthians now darkening Rome's horizon,
The Indian or the Chinese peoples huddled
   Close to the rising run,

Shall, as thy right hand, deal the broad earth justice:
Thy part, above, to make Olympus tremble
With the stern chariot and hurl down angry
   Bolts on polluted groves.

13

'That rosy neck, those smooth and wax-white arms' –
Lydia, when you regale me with Telephus' charms,
Bile boils and chokes me, my mind fails,
Tears – I can't help them – trickle, my cheek pales:
Proof of the slow fires that gnaw at my entrails.

furtim labitur, arguens
quam lentis penitus macerer ignibus.
uror, seu tibi candidos
turparunt umeros immodicae mero
rixae, sive puer furens
impressit memorem dente labris notam.
non, si me satis audias,
speres perpetuum dulcia barbare
laedentem oscula quae Venus
quinta parte sui nectaris imbuit.
felices ter et amplius
quos irrupta tenet copula nec malis
divulsus querimoniis
suprema citius solvet amor die.

XIV

O navis, referent in mare te novi
fluctus! o quid agis? fortiter occupa
portum! nonne vides ut
nudum remigio latus,

et malus celeri saucius Africo,
antennaeque gemant, ac sine funibus
vix durare carinae
possint imperiosius

aequor? non tibi sunt integra lintea,
non di quos iterum pressa voces malo.
quamvis Pontica pinus,
silvae filia nobilis,

And if one of your drunken rows has left scars behind
On your snowy shoulders, or bites furiously signed
On your lips, I burn! But listen to me: you will lose
Your 'faithful' lover, this savage whose kisses bruise
That exquisite mouth which Aphrodite imbues

With her quintessential nectar. A hundredfold
Happy are they alone whom affections hold
Inseparably united; those who stay
Friends without quarrels, and cannot be torn away
From each other's arms until their dying day.

14

Beware, good ship! Fresh squalls are taking
You out to sea again. Start making
 For harbour, run in hard.
 Listen – a groaning yard;

And look – both sides stripped, oars gone, mast
Crippled by the sou'wester's blast.
 The hull can scarcely hope,
 Shorn of its girding-rope,

To ride the ungovernable seas;
Your sails are torn; the images
 To which, hard pressed, you turn
 Have vanished from the stern.

Daughter you may be of a fine
Plantation, true-bred Pontic pine,
 But pride of name and wood
 Will do you little good.

iactes et genus et nomen inutile,
nil pictis timidus navita puppibus
   fidit. tu, nisi ventis
     debes ludibrium, cave.

nuper sollicitum quae mihi taedium,
nunc desiderium curaque non levis,
   interfusa nitentis
     vites aequora Cycladas.

XV

Pastor cum traheret per freta navibus
Idaeis Helenen perfidus hospitam,
   ingrato celeris obruit otio
     ventos, ut caneret fera

Nereus fata: mala ducis avi domum,
quam multo repetet Graecia milite,
   coniurata tuas rumpere nuptias
     et regnum Priami vetus.

heu heu, quantus equis, quantus adest viris
sudor! quanta moves funera Dardanae
   genti! iam galeam Pallas et aegida
     currusque et rabiem parat.

nequiquam Veneris praesidio ferox
pectes caesariem grataque feminis
   imbelli cithara carmina divides,
     nequiquam thalamo gravis

hastas et calami spicula Gnosii
vitabis strepitumque et celerem sequi
   Aiacem; tamen heu serus adulteros
     crines pulvere collines.

No sailor puts his trust in mere
Paintwork in danger.   Good ship, steer
    Wisely – or on a rock
    Be the winds' laughing-stock.

O once my worry and despair,
But now my loving charge and care,
    Avoid the Cyclades:
    Bright islands, treacherous seas.

15

When Paris, the perfidious shepherd boy,
Kidnapped his host's wife and set sail for Troy,
Nereus imposed a calm upon the seas
And checked the eager winds, to utter these
Grim words of prophecy: 'Ill fare you now
That take her homewards whom all Greece shall vow
To get again with armies pledged to undo
Your love-knot – Priam's ancient kingdom too.
Ah, what a terrible sweat of death is brewing
For war-horses and warriors! What huge ruin
You bring your people! I see Pallas getting
Helmet and shield and chariot out, and whetting
Her fury. Serenade admiring girls
On the unwarlike lyre, comb your long curls,
Or, confident of Aphrodite's aid,
Loll in your lover's bedroom and evade
The ponderous spears, the darts of Cretan reed,
Yet death, though late may come the sorry time,
Shall drag your adulterous tresses in the grime.
Have you no visions of the Ithacan,
Troy's executioner, or the old man,
Nestor of Pylos? Fast and furious,
Teucer comes after you, and Sthenelus,
A skilled foot-soldier and, when called to steer,

non Laertiaden, exitium tuae
gentis, non Pylium Nestora respicis?
urgent impavidi te Salaminius
   Teucer, te Sthenelus sciens

pugnae, sive opus est imperitare equis,
non auriga piger. Merionen quoque
nosces, ecce furit te reperire atrox
   Tydides melior patre,

quem tu, cervus uti vallis in altera
visum parte lupum graminis immemor,
sublimi fugies mollis anhelitu,
   non hoc pollicitus tuae.

iracunda diem proferet Ilio
matronisque Phrygum classis Achillei;
post certas hiemes uret Achaicus
   ignis Iliacas domos.

XVI

O matre pulchra filia pulchrior,
quem criminosis cumque voles modum
   pones iambis, sive flamma
     sive mari libet Hadriano.

non Dindymene, non adytis quatit
mentem sacerdotum incola Pythius,
   non Liber aeque, non acuta
     sic geminant Corybantes aera,

tristes ut irae, quas neque Noricus
deterret ensis nec mare naufragum
   nec saevus ignis nec tremendo
     Iuppiter ipse ruens tumultu.

By no means a slow-driving charioteer.
You shall meet Meriones, and also know
That son more famous than his father – lo,
Fierce Diomedes raging on your track ;
Whom you shall run from, gasping, head thrown back
(Was this the scene you promised her in bed ?)
As the poor timid deer, gone from its head
All thoughts of grazing, bolts when it has seen
A wolf at the other end of the ravine.
Achilles' angry faction may delay
Troy's and the Trojan mothers' mourning day,
Yet the predestined count of years must come:
Greek fire shall burn the roofs of Ilium.'

16

O lovely mother's still more lovely daughter,
Those scurrilous iambics I once penned
Dispose of any way you want to: send
Them up in fire or down in deep-sea water.

Not Pythian Phoebus when his priestess trembles
With inspiration in the inner shrine,
Not Phrygian Cybele, not the god of wine,
Not the wild Corybants' shrill-clashing cymbals

Master the soul like bitter rage, which even
Fierce flame or Noric steel cannot deter,
Or the ship-wrecking sea, or Jupiter
Himself plunging in thunder from high heaven.

fertur Prometheus addere principi
limo coactus particulam undique
   desectam et insani leonis
     vim stomacho apposuisse nostro.

irae Thyesten exitio gravi
stravere et altis urbibus ultimae
   stetere causae cur perirent
     funditus imprimeretque muris

hostile aratrum exercitus insolens.
compesce mentem: me quoque pectoris
   temptavit in dulci iuventa
     fervor et in celeris iambos

misit furentem: nunc ego mitibus
mutare quaero tristia, dum mihi
   fias recantatis amica
     opprobriis animumque reddas.

XVII

Velox amoenum saepe Lucretilem
mutat Lycaeo Faunus et igneam
   defendit aestatem capellis
     usque meis pluviosque ventos.

impune tutum per nemus arbutos
quaerunt latentis et thyma deviae
   olentis uxores mariti,
     nec viridis metuunt colubras

nec Martialis haediliae lupos,
utcumque dulci, Tyndari, fistula
   valles et Usticae cubantis
     levia personuere saxa.

Prometheus, forced to take from every creature
Some element to add to the first clay
From which he made man, grafted, so they say,
The ravening lion's violence to our nature.

Rage laid Thyestes' race in grim prostration;
Rage is the clear cause why each tall-towered town
That history tells of was brought toppling down
In ruins, and the arrogant conquering nation

Printed the plough where walls once marked a city.
Do not be angry, then. It was the sweet
Madness of youth that drove me in the heat
Of indignation to dash off that witty

Lampoon. But now my verses shall be changed from
Nasty to nice, if only you'll be friends,
Accept this recantation as amends,
And give me back the heart I've been estranged from.

17

When nimble Faunus needs a change,
He leaves Lycaeus, his home range,
To visit Mount Lucretilis,
Our handsome hill; and while he is
In residence my herd remains
Protected from the winds and rains
And the noon heat. Then far from home
The rank he-goat's hareem can comb
The woods for arbutus and climb
In safety up the banks of thyme.
No venomous green serpent or
Wolf, mascot of the god of war,
Startles my kids once Pan has played
His silver-sounding pipes and made
The smooth-worn rocks and sloping ground
Of low-lying Ustica resound.

di me tuentur, dis pietas mea
et musa cordi est. hic tibi copia
  manabit ad plenum benigno
    ruris honorum opulenta cornu:

hic in reducta valle Caniculae
vitabis aestus et fide Teia
  dices laborantis in uno
    Penelopen vitreamque Circen:

hic innocentis pocula Lesbii
duces sub umbra, nec Semeleius
  cum Marte confundet Thyoneus
    proelia, nec metues protervum

suspecta Cyrum, ne male dispari
incontinentis iniciat manus
  et scindat haerentem coronam
    crinibus immeritamque vestem.

XVIII

Nullam, Vare, sacra vite prius severis arborem
circa mite solum Tiburis et moenia Catili.
siccis omnia nam dura deus proposuit, neque
mordaces aliter diffugiunt sollicitudines.
quis post vina gravem militiam aut pauperiem crepat?
quis non te potius, Bacche pater, teque, decens Venus?
ac ne quis modici transiliat munera Liberi,
Centaurea monet cum Lapithis rixa super mero
debellata, monet Sithoniis non levis Euhius,

The gods watch over me; a heart
That's reverent and the poet's art
Please them. Rich plenty here shall fill
Her horn up to the brim and spill
The harvest's glorious revenue
Liberally, Tyndaris, for you.
Here you may shun the Dog-star's fire,
Vale-sheltered, and upon the lyre
Of Teos sing old songs of sea-
Green Circe and Penelope
(Two women love-sick for one man)
And quench your thirst with Lesbian
Under the shade and take no harm.
Here you need never feel alarm
That Mars and Bacchus may combine
And blows be mixed as well as wine,
Nor shall you be molested by
That lecher with the jealous eye,
Cyrus – for you a sorry match.
Here those rude fingers cannot snatch
At your poor innocent dress or tear
The clinging garland from your hair.

18

Give the sacred vine the preference, Varus, when you plant
   your trees
Round the city walls of Catilus and in Tibur's fertile leas:
For the god has cursed abstainers – nothing in their lives
   goes right;
He alone provides the means to put man-eating cares to flight.
After two cups who complains of debt or serving in the wars?
No; men sing your praises, Father Bacchus, and, sweet
   Venus, yours.
But a word against abusing moderate Liber's bounties: think
How the Centaurs and the Lapiths came to blows and fought
   in drink

cum fas atque nefas exiguo fine libidinum
discernunt avidi. non ego te, candide Bassareu,
invitum quatiam, nec variis obsita frondibus
sub divum rapiam. saeva tene cum Berecyntio
cornu tympana, quae subsequitur caecus Amor sui
et tollens vacuum plus nimio Gloria verticem
arcanique Fides prodiga, perlucidior vitro.

XIX

Mater saeva Cupidinum
Thebanaeque iubet me Semelae puer
    et lasciva Licentia
finitis animum reddere amoribus.
    urit me Glycerae nitor
splendentis Pario marmore purius:
    urit grata protervitas
et vultus nimium lubricus aspici.
    in me tota ruens Venus
Cyprum deseruit, nec patitur Scythas
    et versis animosum equis
Parthum dicere nec quae nihil attinent.
    hic vivum mihi caespitem, hic
verbenas, pueri, ponite turaque
    bimi cum patera meri:
mactata veniet lenior hostia.

To the death, and how the Thracians lose the god's good will
    through wine
When their passions blur and narrow right and wrong's
    dividing-line.
Bright one, I shall never shake you roughly when you're loth
    to play,
Or expose your mystic leaf-veiled emblems to the glare of day.
Bid those Berecynthian horns be silent! Hush the madding
    drum!
In the train of that wild music terrible attendants come –
Blind Self-love; Conceit, her foolish head held high; and
    indiscreet
Trust, as clear as glass and ready-charged with secrets to
    repeat.

19

The Mother of the Loves, unkindly
    Goddess, and Semele's son combine
With wild Abandon to remind me
    That though I had thought desire
    Dead, it still burns. The fire

Is Glycera. She glows more whitely
    Than marble from a Parian mine;
Her sweet audacities delight me;
    That dazzling beauty is
    Love's slippery precipice.

Venus, full-strength, from Cyprus sailing,
    Occupies me. Her law allows
No Scythian wars, no Parthians hailing
    Shafts as their horses turn,
    No theme not her concern.

Bring me fresh altar-turf, slaves! Scatter
    Incense, gather in sacred boughs!
Pour out the new wine in a platter!
    A victim's blood will halt
    The shock of her assault.

XX

Vile potabis modicis Sabinum
cantharis, Graeca quod ego ipse testa
conditum levi, datus in theatro
   cum tibi plausus,

care Maecenas eques, ut paterni
fluminis ripae simul et iocosa
redderet laudes tibi Vaticani
   montis imago.

Caecubum et prelo domitam Caleno
tu bibes uvam: mea nec Falernae
temperant vites neque Formiani
   pocula colles.

XXI

Dianam tenerae dicite virgines,
intonsum, pueri, dicite Cynthium
   Latonamque supremo
     dilectam penitus Iovi.

vos laetam fluviis et nemorum coma,
quaecumque aut gelido prominet Algido
   nigris aut Erymanthi
     silvis aut viridis Cragi.

vos Tempe totidem tollite laudibus
natalemque, mares, Delon Apollinis,
   insignemque pharetra
     fraternaque umerum lyra.

20

My dear Maecenas, noble knight,
You'll drink cheap Sabine here tonight
From common cups. Yet I myself
Sealed it and stored it on the shelf
In a Greek jar that day the applause
Broke out in your recovery's cause,
So that the compliment resounded
Through the full theatre and rebounded
From your own Tiber's banks until
The echo laughed on Vatican hill.
At your house you enjoy the best –
Caecuban or the grape that's pressed
At Cales. But whoever hopes
My cups will taste of Formian slopes
Or of the true Falernian
Must leave a disappointed man.

21

Virgin maidens, praise Diana.
Young men, sing a like hosanna
To the flowing-haired Apollo,
And with adoration follow
Of their mother Leto, nearest
To the heart of Jove, his dearest.
Girls, hymn her who loves all rivers
And the foliage that quivers
Vivid on her chilly height in
Latium, and who takes delight in
Verdant Cragus and pine-sombre
Erymanthus's dark timber.
Boys, give Tempe praise meanwhile and
Delos, the god's birthday island.

hic bellum lacrimosum, hic miseram famem
pestemque a populo et principe Caesare in
   Persas atque Britannos
     vestra motus aget prece.

XXII

Integer vitae scelerisque purus
non eget Mauris iaculis neque arcu
nec venenatis gravida sagittis,
   Fusce, pharetra,

sive per Syrtis iter aestuosas
sive facturus per inhospitalem
Caucasum vel quae loca fabulosus
   lambit Hydaspes.

namque me silva lupus in Sabina,
dum meam canto Lalagen et ultra
terminum curis vagor expeditis,
   fugit inermem,

quale portentum neque militaris
Daunias latis alit aesculetis
nec Iubae tellus generat, leonum
   arida nutrix.

pone me pigris ubi nulla campis
arbor aestiva recreatur aura,
quod latus mundi nebulae malusque
   Iuppiter urget;

Let the lyre too have due mention
(Brother Mercury's invention),
Which beside the arrow-holder
Shines upon Apollo's shoulder.
He'll keep wars and plagues and famines
Far from Caesar and the Romans,
Visiting them on Persians, Dacians,
Britons, all the enemy nations,
Moved by these your supplications.

22

The good man innocent of sin,
Fuscus, may walk the world unharmed.
He has no need to travel armed
With bow or Moorish javelin

Or clanking, poison-arrowed quiver
To cross the Syrtes' burning sands,
The hostile Caucasus or the lands
Washed by that legendary river,

Hydaspes. Proof: quite unconcerned,
Singing of Lalage in my grounds,
I wandered unarmed out of bounds
And when I met a wolf it turned

And fled! Apulia, whose scions
Are soldiers, in broad oakwoods feeds
No beast that size; Numidia breeds,
Parched nurse of monsters, lesser lions.

Banish me to a lifeless plain
Where no tree ever is renewed
By summer's breeze, some latitude
Of louring weather and long rain,

pone sub curru nimium propinqui
solis in terra domibus negata:
dulce ridentem Lalagen amabo,
    dulce loquentem.

XXIII

Vitas inuleo me similis, Chloe,
quaerenti pavidam montibus aviis
    matrem non sine vano
        aurarum et siluae metu.

nam seu mobilibus veris inhorruit
adventus foliis seu virides rubum
    dimovere lacertae,
        et corde et genibus tremit.

atqui non ego te tigris ut aspera
Gaetulusve leo frangere persequor:
    tandem desine matrem
        tempestiva sequi viro.

XXIV

Quis desiderio sit pudor aut modus
tam cari capitis? praecipe lugubris
cantus, Melpomene, cui liquidam pater
    vocem cum cithara dedit.

ergo Quintilium perpetuus sopor
urget! cui Pudor et Iustitiae soror,
incorrupta Fides, nudaque Veritas
    quando ullum inveniet parem?

Or where the sun steers close and mile
On mile is uninhabited heat,
I'll still love Lalage, my sweet
Chatterer with the charming smile.

23

Chloe, you will not venture near,
Just like a lost young mountain deer
Seeking her frantic dam; for her each
Gust in the trees is a needless fear.

Whether the spring-announcing breeze
Shudders the light leaves or she sees
The brambles twitched by a green lizard,
Panic sets racing her heart and knees.

Am I a fierce Gaetulian
Lion or some tiger with a plan
To seize and maul you? Come, now, leave your
Mother: you're ready to know a man.

24

When somebody as dear as he is dead,
Grief must be huge and uninhibited.
Melpomene, to whom, God-given, belong
Lyre and clear voice, teach me a funeral song.
So, now Quintilius sleeps the sleep which men
Never recover from; and who knows when
Honour, Good Faith and naked Truth will find
His parallel again among mankind?

multis ille bonis flebilis occidit,
nulli flebilior quam tibi, Vergili.
tu frustra pius heu non ita creditum
    poscis Quintilium deos.

quid si Threicio blandius Orpheo
auditam moderere arboribus fidem,
num vanae redeat sanguis imagini,
    quam virga semel horrida,

non lenis precibus fata recludere,
nigro compulerit Mercurius gregi?
durum: sed levius fit patientia
    quidquid corrigere est nefas.

XXV

Parcius iunctas quatiunt fenestras
iactibus crebris iuvenes protervi,
nec tibi somnos adimunt, amatque
    ianua limen,

quae prius multum facilis movebat
cardines; audis minus et minus iam
'me tuo longas pereunte noctes,
    Lydia, dormis?'

invicem moechos anus arrogantis
flebis in solo levis angiportu,
Thracio bacchante magis sub inter-
    lunia vento,

cum tibi flagrans amor et libido,
quae solet matres furiare equorum,
saeviet circa iecur ulcerosum,
    non sine questu

He's dead: good men in plenty mourn his end,
But none of them as bitterly, my friend
Virgil, as you, who even now still strain
The power of prayer demanding back, in vain,
Life, which the gods on their terms lend and take.
Though you were Thracian Orpheus and could make
The woods hang listening on your lute, would music
Conjure the blood back to his veins or physic
The sickly ghost once it has passed the gate
Which Mercury, stern officer of Fate,
Shuts against all entreaty, and been made
Of that grim-wanded shepherd's flock a shade?
Loss hurts. Yet patience helps us to endure
The ills no human should presume to cure.

25

The young bloods come round less often now,
Pelting your shutters and making a row
And robbing your beauty sleep. Now the door
Clings lovingly close to the jamb – though, before,

It used to move on its hinge pretty fast.
Those were the days – and they're almost past –
When lovers stood out all night long crying,
'Lydia, wake up! Save me! I'm dying!'

Soon your time's coming to be turned down
And to feel the scorn of the men about town –
A cheap hag haunting alley places
On moonless nights when the wind from Thrace is

Rising and raging, and so is the fire
In your raddled loins, the brute desire
That drives the mothers of horses mad.
You'll be lonely then and complain how sad

laeta quod pubes hedera virenti
gaudeat pulla magis atque myrto,
aridas frondis hiemis sodali
    dedicet Euro.

XXVI

Musis amicus tristitiam et metus
tradam protervis in mare Creticum
    portare ventis, quis sub Arcto
      rex gelidae metuatur orae,

quid Tiridaten terreat, unice
securus. o quae fontibus integris
    gaudes, apricos necte flores,
      necte meo Lamiae coronam,

Piplei dulcis! nil sine te mei
prosunt honores: hunc fidibus novis,
    hunc Lesbio sacrare plectro
      teque tuasque decet sorores.

That the gay young boys enjoy the sheen
Of ivy best or the darker green
Of myrtle: dry old leaves they send
As a gift to the east wind, winter's friend.

26

The Muses love me: I shall throw
My gloom and fears to the winds to blow
   Over the Cretan seas
   Anyhow they please,

Happy to neither know nor care
Which northern king beneath the Bear
   From his frost-bitten shore
   Threatens the world with war,

Or what fresh machinations make
The Parthian Tiridates quake.
   Sweet Muse, to whom the clear
   Pierian founts are dear,

Weave, weave the full-blown summer flowers
For Lamia's head. Yours are the powers
   By which my verse gives fame,
   And Lamia is a name

That you in concert with your eight
Sisters may fitly celebrate
   In my new style – an ode
   In the Alcaic mode.

XXVII

Natis in usum laetitiae scyphis
pugnare Thracum est: tollite barbarum
   morem, verecundumque Bacchum
     sanguineis prohibete rixis.

vino et lucernis Medus acinaces
immane quantum discrepat: impium
   lenite clamorem, sodales,
     et cubito remanete presso.

vultis severi me quoque sumere
partem Falerni? dicat Opuntiae
   frater Megillae, quo beatus
     vulnere, qua pereat sagitta.

cessat voluntas? non alia bibam
mercede. quate te cumque domat Venus,
   non erubescendis adurit
     ignibus, ingenuoque semper

amore peccas. quidquid habes, age
depone tutis auribus. a! miser,
   quanta laborabas Charybdi,
     digne puer meliore flamma.

quae saga, quis te solvere Thessalis
magus venenis, quis poterit deus?
   vix illigatum te triformi
     Pegasus expediet Chimaera.

27

To brawl with cups intended for pleasure is
What men in Thrace do – barbarous habit, to
   Be laid aside. Our modest Bacchus
     Ought to be sheltered from bloody mêlées.

Lamplight and wine make scarcely the setting for
Short Persian dirks drawn drunkenly. Hush, for the
   God's sake less uproar, comrades. Keep your
     Places, your banqueting elbows steady.

I too must down my share of Falernian
Strong wine, you say ? All right; but the brother of
   Lyde from Locris has to tell whose
     Arrow has made him a blissful victim.

He's backing down ? No, those are my drinking terms.
Come, I'm convinced, whoever's enslaved you, there's
   No need to blush: true love has kindled
     Passionate fires, and we know you always

Prefer a freeborn mistress. Then out with it!
Our ears are safe, no matter who . . . Miserable
   Boy, what a whirlpool's dragged you struggling
     Down! You deserve to be better suited.

What witch, what drug-skilled wizard from Thessaly,
What god indeed knows how to release you from
   That triple hell-hound's fatal clutches ?
     Pegasus even could hardly manage.

XXVIII

Te maris et terrae numeroque carentis harenae
    mensorem cohibent, Archyta,
pulveris exigui prope litus parva Matinum
    munera, nec quicquam tibi prodest
aerias temptasse domos animoque rotundum
    percurrisse polum morituro.
occidit et Pelopis genitor, conviva deorum,
    Tithonusque remotus in auras,
et Iovis arcanis Minos admissus, habentque
    Tartara Panthoiden iterum Orco
demissum, quamvis clipeo Troiana refixo
    tempora testatus nihil ultra
nervos atque cutem morti concesserat atrae,
    iudice te non sordidus auctor
naturae verique. sed omnis una manet nox
    et calcanda semel via leti.
dant alios Furiae torvo spectacula Marti;
    exitio est avidum mare nautis;
mixta senum ac iuvenum densentur funera; nullum
    saeva caput Proserpina fugit.
me quoque devexi rapidus comes Orionis
    Illyricis Notus obruit undis.
at tu, nauta, vagae ne parce malignus harenae
    ossibus et capiti inhumato
particulam dare: sic, quodcumque minabitur Eurus
    fluctibus Hesperiis, Venusinae
plectantur silvae te sospite, multaque merces
    unde potest tibi defluat aequo
ab Iove Neptunoque sacri custode Tarenti.
    neglegis immeritis nocituram
postmodo te natis fraudem committere? fors et
    debita iura vicesque superbae
te maneant ipsum: precibus non linquar inultis,
    teque piacula nulla resolvent.

28

Archytas, measurer of earth and ocean,
  Computer of the sea-sands' infinite score,
A little mound, the bare due of devotion,
  Confines you now beside the Matine shore.
In vain you escaladed the aerial
  Ramparts and toured the rondure of the sky
With that great spirit: it was doomed to burial.
  Even Tantalus, the gods' guest, had to die.
Though snatched into the clouds, Aurora's lover
  Tithonus died, and Minos, whom Jove made
His confidant; and, taking him twice over,
  This time Hell keeps Pythagoras as a shade,
Although by choice of shield he proved his claim to
  Have known the epoch of the Trojan war
And yielded nothing but his skin and frame to
  Shadowy Death the time he died before.
No mean authority on truth and nature
  You reckoned him, yet still he met his doom.
One night of darkness waits for every creature;
  One road we tread once only – to the tomb.
Some souls the Furies give to Mars to stage his
  Grim shows; the sea is greedy for more dead;
Pell-mell the corpses jostle, of all ages;
  Cruel Proserpine spares not a single head.
Me too stormy Orion's friend, the driving
  South-wester, drowned in the Illyrian wave.
Sailor, be generous. Do not leave, depriving
  My skull and bones that lie without a grave
Of a few shifting grains. Give, and whatever
  Threats the east winds to the Adriatic roar,
Let the Venusian coastal forests shiver,
  You shall sail safe, and may good profit pour
Into your hands from every lawful quarter –
  From friendly Jove and Neptune, who keeps guard

quamquam festinas, non est mora longa; licebit
iniecto ter pulvere curras.

XXIX

Icci, beatis nunc Arabum invides
gazis, et acrem militiam paras
    non ante devictis Sabaeae
        regibus, horribilique Medo

nectis catenas ? quae tibi virginum
sponso necato barbara serviet ?
    puer quis ex aula capillis
        ad cyathum statuetur unctis,

doctus sagittas tendere Sericas
arcu paterno ? quis neget arduis
    pronos relabi posse rivos
        montibus et Tiberim reverti,

cum tu coemptos undique nobilis
libros Panaeti Socraticam et domum
    mutare loricis Hiberis,
        pollicitus meliora, tendis ?

Over Tarentum's consecrated water.
  Surely you cannot lightly disregard
The harm this sin will bring your unoffending
  Children one day? Who knows, you may be made
The victim of neglect at your own ending,
  Your scorn requited, your last rites unpaid.
Fail, and no sacrifice can make atonement,
  Nor shall I, unavenged, be left to lie.
Friend, check your haste. Pause here one little moment.
  Scatter three handfuls, and you may pass by.

29

    So, Iccius, you're lusting for
    Arabian loot, an all-out war?
      The still recalcitrant
      Emirs of the Levant

    Must bow to Iccius. Iccius leads
    Home chained the terrifying Medes!
      What sweet barbarian
      (Iccius has slain her man)

    Will cater to your conquering taste?
    What young court Ganymede be placed
      Beside your banquet chair
      With perfume-scented hair,

    Taught at a father's knee the craft
    Of archery with the eastern shaft?
      Can anyone discount
      Stories of streams that mount

    Backwards up mountains to their source
    Or Tiber contradicting course,
      When someone like yourself
      Sells up a fine bookshelf –

XXX

O Venus, regina Cnidi Paphique,
sperne dilectam Cypron et vocantis
ture te multo Glycerae decoram
    transfer in aedem.

fervidus tecum puer et solutis
Gratiae zonis properentque Nymphae
et parum comis sine te Iuventas
    Mercuriusque.

XXXI

Quid dedicatum poscit Apollinem
vates ? quid orat de patera novum
    fundens liquorem ? non opimae
        Sardiniae segetes feraces,

non aestuosae grata Calabriae
armenta, non aurum aut ebur Indicum,
    non rura quae Liris quieta
        mordet aqua taciturnus amnis.

premant Calenam falce quibus dedit
fortuna vitem, dives et aureis
    mercator exsiccet culullis
        vina Syra reparata merce,

His Stoic and Socratic rows
Hunted for everywhere – and throws
 Such promise overboard
 For a new Spanish sword?

30

O Queen of Cnidos, Paphos,
 Come, leave, though dearly thine,
Cyprus; for here's thick incense,
 And Glycera calls divine
 Venus to her new shrine.

Bring fiery little Cupid
 And the Nymphs as company.
Bid the loose-girdled Graces
 And, graceless without thee,
 Youth come, and Mercury.

31

What boon, Apollo, what does the poet as
He pours the new wine out of the bowl at your
 New shrine request? Not bumper harvests
  (Prayer of Sardinian millionaires), nor

Huge herds of fine cows grazed in Calabria's
Heat, nor the Far East's goldware and ivory,
 Nor land that Liris, silent river,
  Nibbles away with its sleepy water.

To each his life-work. Let the Calenian
Prune back his vines. Let merchants with moneybags
 Swill out of pure gold cups the wines they
  Buy on the profits from Tyre and Sidon –

dis carus ipsis, quippe ter et quater
anno revisens aequor Atlanticum
   impune. me pascunt olivae,
     me cichorea levesque malvae.

fruit paratis et valido mihi,
Latoe, dones, at, precor, integra
   cum mente, nec turpem senectam
     degere nec cithara carentem.

XXXII

Poscimur. si quid vacui sub umbra
lusimus tecum, quod et hunc in annum
vivat et pluris, age dic Latinum,
   barbite, carmen,

Lesbio primum modulate civi,
qui ferox bello, tamen inter arma
sive iactatam religarat udo
   litore navim,

Liberum et Musas Veneremque et illi
semper haerentem puerum canebat
et Lycum nigris oculis nigroque
   crine decorum.

o decus Phoebi et dapibus supremi
grata testudo Iovis, o laborum
dulce lenimen, mihi cumque salve
   rite vocanti.

God's own elect: how else can they weather the
Atlantic three times yearly and come to port
    Unscathed? For me, though, olives, endives,
        Mallows – the last for a smooth digestion.

Here's what I crave most, son of Latona, then:
Good health, a sound mind, relish of life, and an
    Old age that still maintains a stylish
        Grip on itself and the lyric metres.

32

They want a poem. If we have played
Light-hearted music in the shade
When time hung idle in the past,
Trifles, my lyre, destined to last
One year or many, help me play
Now, to request, a Roman lay –
You whom the Lesbian patriot
First tuned and never once forgot;
For though he hotly drew his sword
On battlefields and, storm-driven, moored
His boat off beaches soaked with brine,
Still he praised Bacchus and the nine
Muses and Venus, at whose side
Cupid clings close, and that dark-eyed,
Dark-haired young Lycus he adored.
Lyre, welcome guest at the high board
Of Jove, Apollo's shining sign
Of godhead, blessed anodyne
Of care – whenever I have made
Due invocation, give me aid.

XXXIII

Albi, no doleas plus nimio memor
immitis Glycerae neu miserabilis
decantes elegos, cur tibi iunior
    laesa praeniteat fide,

insignem tenui fronte Lycorida
Cyri torret amor, Cyrus in asperam
declinat Pholoen; sed prius Apulis
    iungentur capreae lupis,

quam turpi Pholoe peccet adultero.
sin visum Veneri, cui placet imparis
formas atque animos sub iuga aenea
    saevo mittere cum ioco.

ipsum me melior cum peteret Venus,
grata detinuit compede Myrtale
libertina, fretis acrior Hadriae
    curvantis Calabros sinus.

XXXIV

Parcus deorum cultor et infrequens
insanientis dum sapientiae
    consultus erro, nunc retrorsum
        vela dare atque iterare cursus

cogor relictos: namque Diespiter,
igni corusco nubila dividens
    plerumque, per purum tonantis
        egit equos volucremque currum,

33

Tibullus, give up this extravagant grieving
For a sweetheart turned sour. 'Why was she deceiving?'
You ask, and then whimper long elegies on
The theme of the older man being outshone.

Lycoris, whose forehead is nearly all curls,
Is burning for Cyrus. *His* favourite girl's
Pholoe. *She* in turn throws him a frown
Meaning 'Does and Apulian wolves will bed down

Sooner than I'll take a peasant like him!'
That's Venus's method. According to whim
She puts bodies and minds to work her brass yoke
In incongruous pairs – and enjoys the bad joke.

I know. When a far better chance was presented
I stayed with my freed-woman, chained and contented,
Though she handed out stormier treatment to me
Than dented Calabria gets from the sea.

34

I, who have never been
A generous or a keen
Friend of the gods, must now confess
Myself professor in pure foolishness,

And, driven by sheer force
Of proof to alter course,
Must shift my sails and voyage back
To think again upon a different tack.

quo bruta tellus et vaga flumina,
quo Styx et invisi horrida Taenari
   sedes Atlanteusque finis
     concutitur. valet ima summis

mutare et insignem attenuat deus,
obscura premens; hinc apicem rapax
   fortuna cum stridore acuto
     sustulit, hic posuisse gaudet.

XXXV

O diva, gratum quae regis Antium,
praesens vel imo tollere de gradu
   mortale corpus vel superbos
     vertere funeribus triumphos,

te pauper ambit sollicita prece
ruris colonus, te dominam aequoris
   quicumque Bithyna lacessit
     Carpathium pelagus carina.

te Dacus asper, te profugi Scythae,
urbesque gentesque et Latium ferox
   regumque matres barbarorum et
     purpurei metuunt tyranni,

For Jove, who usually throws
A lightning-flash that goes
Glittering through intervening cloud,
This morning hurtled with his thunder-loud

Chariot and horses through
A sky entirely blue.
The brute earth and its restless waters,
Styx and the hateful underworld's grim quarters,

Even the last known land
Where Atlas takes his stand
Staggered. I see, then, that God can
Change high and low: the unregarded man

Steps up, the proud backs down.
Here Fortune sets the crown,
But there swoops on her noisy wing
Happy to snatch it from another king.

35

O goddess ruling over favoured Antium,
With power to raise our perishable bodies
    From low degree or turn
The pomp of triumph into funeral,

Thee the poor farmer with his worried prayer
Propitiates; thee, mistress of the ocean,
    Whoever dares the seas
Round Crete in a Bithynian-timbered boat

Entreats; thee wandering Scythian, savage Dacian,
All cities, peoples, even Rome's fierce children
    Dread, and the purple-clad
Despot and mothers of barbarian kings,

iniurioso ne pede proruas
stantem columnam, neu populus frequens
　　ad arma cessantis, ad arma
　　　　concitet imperiumque frangat.

te semper anteit serva Necessitas,
clavos trabalis et cuneos manu
　　gestans aena, nec severus
　　　　uncus abest liquidumque plumbum.

te Spes et albo rara Fides colit
velata panno, nec comitem abnegat,
　　utcumque mutata potentis
　　　　veste domos inimica linquis.

at vulgus infidum et meretrix retro
periura cedit, diffugiunt cadis
　　cum faece siccatis amici
　　　　ferre iugum pariter dolosi.

serves iturum Caesarem in ultimos
orbis Britannos et iuvenum recens
　　examen Eois timendum
　　　　partibus Oceanoque rubro.

eheu, cicatricum et sceleris pudet
fratrumque. quid nos dura refugimus
　　aetas? quid intactum nefasti
　　　　liquimus? unde manum iuventus

metu deorum continuit? quibus
pepercit aris? o utinam nova
　　incude diffingas retusum in
　　　　Massagetas Arabasque ferrum!

Lest thou should'st rudely kick aside the pillar
That props the State, and the mob, rioting, rally
   The waverers with the cry
'To arms, to arms!' and topple government.

Before thee stalks Necessity, thy servant,
Who in her brazen hand grips the strong wedges
   And nails, and with them brings
Her molten lead, her unrelenting clamp.

Close by walks Hope, and white-cloaked Loyalty, seldom
Seen among men – she does not grudge her presence
   When in the garb of grief
Thou turn'st thy face away from the great house.

But the false whore and the fair-weather fellow
Scatter, for when the barrels are drained empty
   Friends, like the wine, run out,
Shirkers in sorrow's harness, not true mates.

Guard Caesar bound for Britain at the world's end,
Guard our young swarm of warriors on the wing now
   To spread the fear of Rome
Into Arabia and the Red Sea coasts.

Alas, the shameful past – our scars, our crimes, our
Fratricides! This hardened generation
   Has winced at nothing, left
No horror unexplored. What profanations

Has fear of heaven kept our young men's hands from?
What altars have they spared? O on fresh anvils
   Reforge our blunted swords
To point at Caspian and Arab hearts!

XXXVI

Et ture et fidibus iuvat
placare et vituli sanguine debito
   custodes Numidae deos,
qui nunc Hesperia sospes ab ultima
   caris multa sodalibus,
nulli plura tamen dividit oscula
   quam dulci Lamiae, memor
actae non alio rege puertiae
   mutataeque simul togae.
Cressa ne careat pulchra dies nota,
   neu promptae modus amphorae,
neu morem in Salium sit requies pedum,
   neu multi Damalis meri
Bassum Threicia vincat amystide,
   neu desint epulis rosae
neu vivax apium neu breve lilium.
   omnes in Damalin putris
deponent oculos, nec Damalis novo
   divelletur adultero
lascivis hederis ambitiosior.

36

Incense and bull's blood and plucked strings –
We owe the gods these offerings
For having safely brought our guest
Of honour back from the far West,
Our Numida. All his close friends here
Get kisses, but he gives his dear
Lamia the most, who shared at school
The same pedagogue-tyrant's rule
And with him in the manhood rite
Changed the dark toga for the white.
Chalk it up on the calendar –
A lucky day! Bring out the jar
Of wine and let it pass about
Without reluctance; and without
A pause for resting, dancers, keep
On dancing with the Salian leap.
Let Damalis, the girl we crown
Champion drinker, be put down
By Bassus at the game of sinking
A whole cup without breath or blinking.
Go, fetch in lilies that fade fast,
Parsley to make the garlands last,
And roses. Soon all eyes shall turn
And languishingly melt and burn
For Damalis. But she won't part
From Numida, her new sweetheart,
And clings more lovingly to him
Than ivy round an ilex limb.

XXXVII

Nunc est bibendum, nunc pede libero
pulsanda tellus, nunc Saliaribus
　　ornare pulvinar deorum
　　　　tempus erat dapibus, sodales.

antehac nefas depromere Caecubum
cellis avitis, dum Capitolio
　　regina dementis ruinas
　　　　funus et imperio parabat

contaminato cum grege turpium
morbo virorum, quidlibet impotens
　　sperare fortunaque dulci
　　　　ebria. sed minuit furorem

vix una sospes navis ab ignibus,
mentemque lymphatam Mareotico
　　redegit in veros timores
　　　　Caesar ab Italia volantem

remis adurgens, accipiter velut
mollis columbas aut leporem citus
　　venator in campis nivalis
　　　　Haemoniae, daret ut catenis

fatale monstrum; quae generosius
perire quaerens nec muliebriter
　　expavit ensem nec latentis
　　　　classe cita reparavit oras;

ausa et iacentem visere regiam
vultu sereno, fortis et asperas
　　tractare serpentis, ut atrum
　　　　corpore combiberet venenum,

37

Today is the day to drink and dance on. Dance, then,
Merrily, friends, till the earth shakes. Now let us
   Rival the priests of Mars
With feasts to deck the couches of the gods.

Not long ago it would have been high treason
To fetch the Caecuban from family store-rooms,
   When the wild Queen was still
Plotting destruction to our Capitol

And ruin to the Empire with her squalid
Pack of diseased half-men – mad, wishful grandeur,
   Tipsy with sweet good luck!
But all her fleet burnt, scarcely one ship saved –

That tamed her rage; and Caesar, when his galleys
Chased her from Italy, soon brought her, dreaming
   And drugged with native wine,
Back to the hard realities of fear.

As swiftly as the hawk follows the feeble
Dove, or in snowy Thessaly the hunter
   The hare, so he sailed forth
To bind this fatal prodigy in chains.

Yet she preferred a finer style of dying:
She did not, like a woman, shirk the dagger
   Or seek by speed at sea
To change her Egypt for obscurer shores,

But, gazing on her desolated palace
With a calm smile, unflinchingly laid hands on
   The angry asps until
Her veins had drunk the deadly poison deep,

deliberata morte ferocior,
saevis Liburnis scilicet invidens
   privata deduci superbo
      non humilis mulier triumpho.

XXXVIII

Persicos odi, puer, apparatus,
displicent nexae philyra coronae;
mitte sectari, rosa quo locorum
   sera moretur.

simplici myrto nihil allabores
sedulus curo: neque te ministrum
dedecet myrtus neque me sub arta
   vite bibentem.

And, death-determined, fiercer then than ever,
Perished. Was she to grace a haughty triumph,
  Dethroned, paraded by
The rude Liburnians? Not Cleopatra!

38

Boy, I detest the Persian style
Of elaboration. Garlands bore me
Laced up with lime-bark. Don't run a mile
To find the last rose of summer for me.

None of your fussy attempts to refine
On simple myrtle. Myrtle suits both
You pouring, me drinking, wine
Under the trellised vine's thick growth.

Q
HORATI
FLACCI
CARMINUM
LIBER SECUNDUS

THE ODES OF
HORACE
BOOK
TWO

I

Motum ex Metello consule civicum
bellique causas et vitia et modos
   ludumque Fortunae gravisque
     principum amicitias et arma

nondum expiatis uncta cruoribus,
periculosae plenum opus aleae,
   tractas, et incedis per ignis
     suppositos cineri doloso.

paulum severae Musa tragoediae
desit theatris: mox ubi publicas
   res ordinaris, grande munus
     Cecropio repetes cothurno,

insigne maestis praesidium reis
et consulenti, Pollio, curiae,
   cui laurus aeternos honores
     Delmatico peperit triumpho.

iam nunc minaci murmure cornuum
perstringis auris, iam litui strepunt,
   iam fulgor armorum fugaces
     terret equos equitumque vultus.

audire magnos iam videor duces
non indecoro pulvere sordidos,
   et cuncta terrarum subacta
     praeter atrocem animum Catonis.

Iuno et deorum quisquis amicior
Afris inulta cesserat impotens
   tellure victorum nepotes
     rettulit inferias Iugurthae.

1

Your theme is civil warfare since Metellus
Was consul. To describe its causes, phases
   And crimes, Fortune's caprice,
The doomed alliances of triumvirs,

The blood-smeared weapons still unexpiated,
Is to traverse a field sown thick with hazards,
   Pollio: you tread on fire
Still smouldering underneath deceptive ash.

Yet do not leave our theatre long deserted
By your stern tragic Muse. Soon, when the history
   Is ordered on the page,
Renew your high vocation, don again

The Attic buskin – you whom the despairing
Defendant and the pondering Senate lean on,
   You whom the laurel brought
Long-lasting glory in Dalmatia's war.

So now you batter our ear-drums with alarums
Blared from the ominous horn and clarion; arms flash
   And horses panic; fear
Quivers reflected in the rider's face.

I have a vision of the great commanders
Jacketed in grime, their uniform of honour,
   And of a world subdued
Except for Cato's unforgiving soul.

Now Juno and the gods who once befriended
The Africans but had no power to save them
   Reap their revenge and lay
The victors' grandsons at Jugurtha's tomb

quis non Latino sanguine pinguior
campus sepulcris impia proelia
   testatur auditumque Medis
      Hesperiae sonitum ruinae?

qui gurges aut quae flumina lugubris
ignara belli? quod mare Dauniae
   non decoloravere caedes?
      quae caret ora cruore nostro?

sed ne relictis, Musa procax, iocis
Ceae retractes munera neniae,
   mecum Dionaeo sub antro
      quaere modos leviore plectro.

II

Nullus argento color est avaris
abdito terris, inimice lamnae
   Crispe Sallusti, nisi temperato
      splendeat usu.

vivet extento Proculeius aevo,
notus in fratres animia paterni;
illum aget penna metuente solvi
   Fama superstes.

latius regnes avidum domando
spiritum, quam si Libyam remotis
Gadibus iungas et uterque Poenus
   serviat uni.

crescit indulgens sibi dirus hydrops,
nec sitim pellit, nisi causa morbi
fugerit venis et aquosus albo
   corpore languor.

As sacrifice. Our fields are rich with Roman
Dead and not one lacks graves to speak against our
   Impious battles. Even
Parthia can hear the ruin of the West.

What lake or river has not had a taste of
Sorrowful war? Our seas are all discoloured
   By slaughter; every beach
Is redder for the spilling of our blood.

Steady, wild Muse! Have you forsworn your light touch?
Simonides wrote better dirges. Come, let's
   Go to the cave of love
And look for music in a jollier key.

2

Sallustius Crispus, you're no friend of metal
Unless it's made to gleam with healthy motion.
Take silver: it becomes lacklustre lying
   Banked in the greedy earth.

The generosity of Proculeius
In acting like a father to his brothers
Outlives him. Everlasting Fame's unflagging
   Wing shall uphold his worth.

Govern your appetites: thereby you'll rule more
Than if you merged Libya with distant Gades
And made the Carthaginians of both countries
   Slaves of a single state.

Greed, when indulged, grows like the savage dropsy:
The thirst sticks close until the veins are rid of
The infection and the pallid, weary body
   Parts with the water's weight.

redditum Cyri solio Phraaten
dissidens plebi numero beatorum
eximit Virtus, populumque falsis
   dedocet uti

vocibus, regnum et diadema tutum
deferens uni propriamque laurum,
quisquis ingentis oculo irretorto
   spectat acervos.

III

Aequam memento rebus in arduis
servare mentem, non secus in bonis
   ab insolenti temperatam
     laetitia, moriture Delli,

seu maestus omni tempore vixeris,
seu te in remoto gramine per dies
   festos reclinatum bearis
     interiore nota Falerni.

quo pinus ingens albaque populus
umbram hospitalem consociare amant
   ramis ? quid obliquo laborat
     lympha fugax trepidare rivo ?

huc vina et unguenta et nimium brevis
flores amoenae ferre iube rosae,
   dum res et aetas et sororum
     fila trium patiuntur atra.

cedes coemptis saltibus et domo
villaque flavus quam Tiberis lavit;
   cedes, et exstructis in altum
     divitiis potietur heres.

Phraates has regained the throne of Cyrus,
But when the populace account him therefore
Happy, Wisdom dissents. She disabuses
　　Men when they misapply

Words. To one man she grants true power, the abiding
Diadem, the inalienable laurel:
He who can pass great heaps of treasure, yet not
　　Swivel a longing eye.

3

Maintain an unmoved poise in adversity;
Likewise in luck one free of extravagant
　　Joy. Bear in mind my admonition,
　　　　Dellius. Whether you pass a lifetime

Prostrate with gloom, or whether you celebrate
Feast-days with choice old brands of Falernian
　　Stretched out in some green, unfrequented
　　　　Meadow, remember your death is certain.

For whom but us do silvery poplar and
Tall pine conspire such welcome with shadowy
　　Laced boughs? Why else should eager water
　　　　Bustle and work in its zigzag channel?

Come, bid them bring wine, perfume and beautiful
Rose-blooms that die too swiftly: be quick while the
　　Dark threads the three grim Sisters weave still
　　　　Hold and your years and the times allow it.

Soon farewell town house, country estate by the
Brown Tiber washed, chain-acres of pasture-land,
　　Farewell the sky-high piles of treasure
　　　　Left with the rest for an heir's enjoyment.

divesne prisco natus ab Inacho
nil interest an pauper et infima
    de gente sub divo moreris,
        victima nil miserantis Orci.

omnes eodem cogimur, omnium
versatur urna serius ocius
    sors exitura et nos in aeternum
        exsilium impositura cumbae.

IV

Ne sit ancillae tibi amor pudori,
Xanthia Phoceu, prius insolentem
    serva Briseis niveo colore
        movit Achillem;

movit Aiacem Telamone natum
forma captivae dominum Tecmessae;
arsit Atrides medio in triumpho
    virgine rapta,

barbarae postquam cecidere turmae
Thessalo victore et ademptus Hector
tradidit fessis leviora tolli
    Pergama Grais.

nescias an te generum beati
Phyllidis flavae decorent parentes:
regium certe genus et penatis
    maeret iniquos.

crede non illam tibi de scelesta
plebe delectam, neque sic fidelem,
sic lucro aversam potuisse nasci
    matre pudenda.

Rich man or poor man, scion of Inachus
Or beggar wretch lodged naked and suffering
   God's skies – it's all one. You and I are
    Victims of never-relenting Orcus,

Sheep driven deathward. Sooner or later Fate's
Urn shakes, the lot comes leaping for each of us
   And books a one-way berth in Charon's
    Boat on the journey to endless exile.

4

Dear Phocian Xanthias, don't feel ashamed
Of loving a servant. The same passion tamed
High and mighty Achilles before you – he gave
His heart to Briseis, his snowy-skinned slave;

The beauty of Trojan Tecmessa enraptured
Her Ajax – the captor it was who was captured;
Agamemnon fired Troy, but the conqueror burned
In his turn for the virgin his victory earned

When Thessaly's Myrmidons carried the day
And the northerners' regiments wilted away,
And Hector was needed and dead, and tall Troy
Light work for the war-weary Greeks to destroy.

For all you know, yellow-haired Phyllis can muster
Proud parents and marriage may add to your lustre;
Her family's undoubtedly royal; perhaps
She's mourning some palace's cruel collapse.

The girl of your choosing could never have come,
I assure you, from low proletarian scum:
Such a loyal, unmercenary heart couldn't go
With a mother you'd be too embarrassed to know.

bracchia et vultum teretesque suras
integer laudo; fuge suspicari
cuius octavum trepidavit aetas
   claudere lustrum.

V

Nondum subacta ferre iugum valet
cervice, nondum munia comparis
   aequare nec tauri ruentis
     in venerem tolerare pondus.

circa virentis est animus tuae
compos iuvencae, nunc fluviis gravem
   solantis aestum, nunc in udo
     ludere cum vitulis salicto

praegestientis. tolle cupidinem
immitis uvae: iam tibi lividos
   distinguet Autumnus racemos
     purpureo varius colore.

iam te sequetur: currit enim ferox
aetas et illi quos tibi dempserit
   apponet annos; iam proterva
     fronte petit Lalage maritum,

dilecta quantum non Pholoe fugax,
non Chloris albo sic umero nitens
   ut pura nocturno renidet
     luna mari, Cnidiusve Gyges,

Those arms and that face and those perfectly turned
Neat ankles are exquisite. Don't look concerned:
Now that Time has run off with my fortieth year
My motives are pure and my praise is sincere.

5

She is not strong enough to bow
Her neck beneath the double plough
Of marriage yet, or tolerate
The shock of the plunging bull's gross weight.

All her mind on green meadows runs.
So longs only to foil the sun's
Sultry oppression in the shallows
Or frisk among the marshy sallows

With her calf-friends. Those grapes are crude:
Deny yourself. Soon dapple-hued
Autumn will give you the ripe cluster
Tinged with the true dark-purple lustre.

Time in his furious career
Will credit her with each fresh year
He takes from you. Soon she will hunt
A mate, soon with a shameless front

Chase you, and be more doted on
Than Chloris was whose white neck shone
Like a clear moon in the night sea,
Or unapproachable Pholoe,

quem si puellarum insereres choro,
mire sagaces falleret hospites
    discrimen obscurum solutis
        crinibus ambiguoque vultu.

VI

Septimi, Gadis aditure mecum et
Cantabrum indoctum iuga ferre nostra et
barbaras Syrtis, ubi Maura semper
    aestuat unda,

Tibur Argeo positum colono
sit meae sedes utinam senectae,
sit modus lasso maris et viarum
    militiaeque!

unde si Parcae prohibent iniquae,
dulce pellitis ovibus Galaesi
flumen et regnata petam Laconi
    rura Phalantho.

ille terrarum mihi praeter omnis
angulus ridet, ubi non Hymetto
mella decedunt viridique certat
    baca Venafro.

ver ubi longum tepidasque praebet
Iuppiter brumas, et amicus Aulon
fertili Baccho minimum Falernis
    invidet uvis.

Or Cnidian Gyges whose long curls
And boy-girl face would, if the girls
Sat round him, thoroughly perplex
A shrewd guest asked to tell his sex.

6

Septimius, my beloved friend,
Who'd go with me to the world's end,
To Gades, or to northern Spain
Still chafing at the imperial rein,
Or to the barbarous terrain
Of Syrtes where the Moorish sea
Hollows and heaves incessantly –
May Tibur, which the pioneers
From Argos built, be my last years'
Haven, a halt for one footsore
From marching, sailing, waging war.
If unkind Fate denies me this
Resting-place, then my next choice is
Galaesus, which the leather-coated
Prize sheep for which the region's noted
Love for sweet water, and the plain
Phalanthus had for his domain –
To me the bonniest square miles
In all the world, a coast of smiles,
Where bees make honeycombs so sweet,
Hymettus has to own defeat,
And even the olives vie with those
That silvery-green Venafrum grows;
Jupiter regularly brings

ille te mecum locus et beatae
postulant arces; ibi tu calentem
debita sparges lacrima favillam
    vatis amici.

VII

O saepe mecum tempus in ultimum
deducte Bruto militiae duce,
    quis te redonavit Quiritem
        dis patriis Italoque caelo,

Pompei, meorum prime sodalium?
cum quo morantem saepe diem mero
    fregi coronatus nitentis
        malobathro Syrio capillos.

tecum Philippos et celerem fugam
sensi relicta non bene parmula,
    cum fracta virtus, et minaces
        turpe solum tetigere mento.

sed me per hostis Mercurius celer
denso paventem sustulit aere;
    te rursus in bellum resorbens
        unda fretis tulit aestuosis.

ergo obligatam redde Iovi dapem
longaque fessum militia latus
    depone sub lauru mea, nec
        parce cadis tibi destinatis.

Mild winters and long, lingering springs,
And Bacchus holds the vines so dear,
Rich Aulon need not sourly fear
Falernum. Come, the place invites
Us both, Tarentum's happy heights
Beckon us. There, when I am dead,
On the warm ashes you shall shed
My due of tears to mark the end
Of Horace, poet and good friend.

7

Pompeius, chief of all my friends, with whom
I often ventured to the edge of doom
   When Brutus led our line,
   With whom, aided by wine

And garlands and Arabian spikenard,
I killed those afternoon that died so hard –
   Who has new-made you, then,
   A Roman citizen

And given you back your native gods and weather?
We two once beat a swift retreat together
   Upon Philippi's field,
   When I dumped my poor shield,

And courage cracked, and the strong men who frowned
Fiercest were felled, chins to the miry ground.
   But I, half-dead with fear,
   Was wafted, airborne, clear

Of the enemy lines, wrapped in a misty blur
By Mercury, not sucked back, as you were,
   From safety and the shore
   By the wild tide of war.

oblivioso levia Massico
ciboria exple; funde capacibus
   unguenta de conchis. quis udo
     deproperare apio coronas

curatve myrto? quem Venus arbitrum
dicet bibendi? non ego sanius
   bacchabor Edonis: recepto
     dulce mihi furere est amico.

VIII

Ulla si iuris tibi peierati
poena, Barine, nocuisset umquam,
dente si nigro fieres vel uno
   turpior ungui,

crederem. sed tu, simul obligasti
perfidum votis caput, enitescis
pulchrior multo iuvenumque prodis
   publica cura.

expedit matris cineres opertos
fallere et toto taciturna noctis
signa cum caelo gelidaque divos
   morte carentis.

Pay Jove his feast, then. In my laurel's shade
Stretch out the bones that long campaigns have made
   Weary. Your wine's been waiting
   For years: no hesitating!

Fill up the polished goblets to the top
With memory-drowning Massic! Slave, unstop
   The deep-mouthed shells that store
   Sweet-smelling oil and pour!

Who'll run to fit us out with wreaths and find
Myrtle and parsley. damp and easily twined?
   Who'll win the right to be
   Lord of the revelry

By dicing highest? I propose to go
As mad as a Thracian. It's sheer joy to throw
   Sanity overboard
   When a dear friend's restored.

8

    Barine, if for perjured truth
    Some punishment had ever hurt you –
    One blemished nail or blackened tooth –
    I might believe this show of virtue.

    But when you stake that head of hair
    On oath, it actually enhances
    Your beauty; all the young men stare
    And you walk on, caressed by glances.

    'Upon my mother's ashes!' 'By
    The silent stars, witness all heaven!'
    'Ye gods beyond cold death!' – each lie
    Improves you somehow. Damn it, even

ridet hoc, inquam, Venus ipsa, rident
simplices Nymphae, ferus et Cupido,
semper ardentis acuens sagittas
    cote cruenta.

adde quod pubes tibi crescit omnis,
servitus crescit nova, nec priores
impiae tectum dominae relinquunt.
    saepe minati.

te suis matres metuunt iuvencis,
te senes parci, miseraeque nuper
virgines nuptae, tua ne redardet
    aura maritos.

IX

Non semper imbres nubibus hispidos
manant in agros aut mare Caspium
    vexant inaequales procellae
      usque, nec Armeniis in oris,

amice Valgi, stat glacies iners
mensis per omnis aut Aquilonibus
    querqueta Gargani laborant
      et foliis viduantur orni:

tu semper urges flebilibus modis
Mysten ademptum, nec tibi Vespero
    surgente decedunt amores
      nec rapidum fugiente solem.

Venus, the Nymphs (dear guileless hearts)
And cruel Cupid busy filing
On the blood-spattered stone the darts
That kindle fire, cannot help smiling.

Meanwhile our boys are held in thrall,
A fresh slave generation's growing,
While the old victims in your hall
Still stay for all their threats of going.

Mean fathers fear, fond mothers fret
For sons, and wretched new brides worry
Lest their home-sailing husbands, met
By your spice wind, forget to hurry.

9

The clouds disgorge a flood
Of rain; fields are churned mud;
   The Caspian seas
Are persecuted by the pouncing blasts;
But, Valgius, my friend, no weather lasts

For ever. Numb ice chokes
Armenia, the oaks
   On Garganus freeze
And groan in the gale, the ash-trees lose their leaves;
Yet nothing natural all the year round grieves.

Why, then, should you prolong
Your elegiac song
   For Mystes? He is dead.
Hesperus rises and the racing sun
Routs him each day, and still you have not done

at non ter aevo functus amabilem
ploravit omnis Antilochum senex
   annos, nec impubem parentes
     Troilon aut Phrygiae sorores

flevere semper. desine mollium
tandem querelarum, et potius nova
   cantemus Augusti tropaea
     Caesaris et rigidum Niphaten,

Medumque flumen gentibus additum
victis minores volvere vertices,
   intraque praescriptum Gelonos
     exiguis equitare campis.

X·

Rectius vives, Licini, neque altum
semper urgendo neque, dum procellas
cautus horrescis, nimium premendo
   litus iniquum.

auream quisquis mediocritatem
diligit tutus, caret obsoleti
sordibus tecti, caret invidenda
   sobrius aula.

saepius ventis agitatur ingens
pinus et celsae graviore casu
decidunt turres feriuntque summos
   fulgura montis.

With grief. Though ninety years
Lay on him, Nestor's tears
   Were not long shed
For dear Antilochus, nor did the clan
Of princely Troilus mourn for their young man

A lifetime. Come, dispense
With these weak-kneed laments
   And let our theme
Be the new victories in the Persian snows
Won by Augustus, how Euphrates flows

Less full of its own foam
Now that it too pays Rome
   A tribute stream,
And the Geloni use a tighter rein,
Penned by the frontiers of their shrunken plain.

10

Licinius, to live wisely shun
The deep sea; on the other hand,
Straining to dodge the storm don't run
Too close in to the jagged land.

All who love safety make their prize
The golden mean and hate extremes:
Mansions are envied for their size,
Slums pitied for their rotting beams.

The loftiest pines, when the wind blows,
Are shaken hardest; tall towers drop
With the worst crash; the lightning goes
Straight to the highest mountain-top.

sperat infestis, metuit secundis
alteram sortem bene praeparatum
pectus. informis hiemes reducit
    Iuppiter, idem

summovet. non, si male nunc, et olim
sic erit: quondam cithara tacentem
suscitat Musam neque semper arcum
    tendit Apollo.

rebus angustis animosus atque
fortis appare; sapienter idem
contrahes vento nimium secundo
    turgida vela.

XI

Quid bellicosus Cantaber et Scythes,
Hirpine Quincti, cogitet Hadria
    divisus obiecto, remittas
        quaerere, nec trepides in usum

poscentis aevi pauca: fugit retro
levis iuventas et decor, arida
    pellente lascivos amores
        canitie facilemque somnum.

non semper idem floribus est honor
vernis, neque uno Luna rubens nitet
    vultu: quid aeternis minorem
        consiliis animum fatigas?

cur non sub alta vel platano vel hac
pinu iacentes sic temere et rosa
    canos odorati capillos,
        dum licet, Assyriaque nardo

Hopeful in trial, shy in success,
The seasoned heart knows luck will swing:
Jove brings foul weather, nonetheless
He soon supplants it with sweet spring.

If things go ill now, before long
They'll mend again. On certain days
The bow lies slack, the sleeping song
Wakes in the lyre, Apollo plays.

When hardship comes, show a brave mind
And a bold face; but when the gale
Follows too fawningly behind,
Be prudent, reef the bulging sail.

11

'Is warlike Spain hatching a plot?'
You ask me anxiously. 'And what
Of Scythia?' My dear Quinctius,
There's a whole ocean guarding us.
Stop fretting: life has simple needs.
Behind us smooth-cheeked youth recedes,
Good looks go too, and in our beds
Dry wizened skins and grizzled heads
Wait to put easy sleep to rout
And drive love's sensuous pleasures out.
Buds lose their springtime gloss, and soon
The full becomes the thin-faced moon.
Futurity is infinite:
Why tax the brain with plans for it?
Better by this tall plane or pine
To sprawl and, while we may, drink wine
And grace with Syrian balsam drops
And roses these fast-greying tops.
Bacchus shoos off the wolves of worry.

potamus uncti ? dissipat Euhius
curas edaces. quis puer ocius
   restinguet ardentis Falerni
      pocula praetereunte lympha ?

quis devium scortum eliciet domo
Lyden ? eburna dic age cum lyra
   maturet in comptum Lacaenae
      more comas religata nodum.

XII

Nolis longa ferae bella Numantiae
nec durum Hannibalem nec Siculum mare
Poeno purpureum sanguine mollibus
   aptari citharae modis,

nec saevos Lapithas et nimium mero
Hylaeum domitosque Herculea manu
Telluris iuvenes, unde periculum
   fulgens contremuit domus

Saturni veteris; tuque pedestribus
dices historiis proelia Caesaris,
Maecenas, melius ductaque per vias
   regum colla minacium.

me dulces dominae Musa Licymniae
cantus, me voluit dicere lucidum
fulgentis oculos et bene mutuis
   fidum pectus amoribus,

quam nec ferre pedem dedecuit choris
nec certare ioco nec dare bracchia
ludentem nitidis virginibus sacro
   Dianae celebris die.

Ho, slaves! Which one of you will hurry
Down to the nearby brook to tame
The heat of this Falernian's flame?
Who'll coax from home to join our feast
Lyde, of easy girls the least
Easy to get? Bid her bestir
Herself and bring along with her
The ivory lyre, wearing her curls
Neat-braided like a Spartan girl's.

12

The history of the long Numantian war;
Iron Hannibal; the sea incarnadined
Off Sicily with Carthaginian gore;
  Wild Lapiths fighting blind-

Drunk Centaurs; or the Giants who made the bright
Halls of old Saturn reel till Hercules
Tamed them – you'd find my gentle lyre too slight
  An instrument for these

Magnificent themes, Maecenas. You can treat
Of Caesar's battles and once bellicose
Chieftains paraded haltered through the street
  Better than I: plain prose

Is called for. My instruction from the Muse is
To sing of your Licymnia's sweet voice,
Her sparkling eyes, and the true heart that chooses
  You and is your dear choice –

A girl who whether she joins the choral dancers,
Or walks with the festal maidens arm-in-arm
On Diana's crowded holy-day, or answers
  A jest, does it with charm.

num tu quae tenuit dives Achaemenes
aut pinguis Phrygiae Mygdonias opes
permutare velis crine Licymniae,
   plenas aut Arabum domos,

cum flagrantia detorquet ad oscula
cervicem aut facili saevitia negat,
quae poscente magis gaudeat eripi,
   interdum rapere occupet?

XIII

Ille et nefasto te posuit die
quicumque primum, et sacrilega manu
   produxit, arbos, in nepotum
      perniciem opprobriumque pagi;

illum et parentis crediderim sui
fregisse cervicem et penetralia
   sparsisse nocturno cruore
      hospitis; ille venena Colcha

et quidquid usquam concipitur nefas
tractavit, agro qui statuit meo
   te triste lignum, te caducum
      in domini caput immerentis.

quid quisque vitet numquam homini satis
cautum est in horas: navita Bosphorum
   Poenus perhorrescit neque ultra
      caeca timet aliunde fata;

miles sagittas et celerem fugam
Parthi, catenas Parthus et Italum
   robur; sed improvisa leti
      vis rapuit rapietque gentis.

The wealth of Achaemenes, the Phrygian earth
That made King Midas rich, the Arab lairs
Bursting with treasure – would you rate them worth
   A single one of her hairs

When she bends her neck to your burning mouth? Resist
Soft-stubbornly she may, but even your thirst
To kiss is less than hers is to be kissed,
   And sometimes she drinks first.

13

Whoever was the first to plant you, tree,
   Did it on a black day; those impious hands
Trained you to massacre posterity
   And bring disgrace upon our local lands.

I can imagine him – a homicide
   Who'd strangled his own father, stabbed a guest
At night and smeared the hearth with blood, applied
   The Colchic poisons, in a word professed

Every abomination that one could
   Conceive of. Last, he placed you on my farm
To topple, miserable lump of wood,
   Onto a master who deserves no harm.

No man is hourly armed against surprise.
   The Carthaginian pilot who takes care
Passing the Bosphorus, forgets what lies
   Beyond, and runs on hidden dooms elsewhere.

When Parthians flee, the legions are afraid
   Of arrows; Parthians fear the captor's chain,
The strength of Rome; but death's an ambuscade
   That has destroyed the world and shall again.

quam paene furvae regna Proserpinae
et iudicantem vidimus Aeacum
    sedesque discriptas piorum et
        Aeoliis fidibus querentem

Sappho puellis de popularibus,
et te sonantem plenius aureo,
    Alcaee, plectro dura navis,
        dura fugae mala, dura belli!

utrumque sacro digna silentio
mirantur umbrae dicere; sed magis
    pugnas et exactos tyrannos
        densum umeris bibit aure vulgus.

quid mirum, ubi illis carminibus stupens
demittit atras belua centiceps
    auris et intorti capillis
        Eumenidum recreantur angues?

quin et Prometheus et Pelopis parens
dulci laborem decipitur sono,
    nec curat Orion leones
        aut timidos agitare lyncas.

XIV

Eheu fugaces, Postume, Postume,
labuntur anni nec pietas moram
    rugis et instanti senectae
        adferet indomitaeque morti:

non si trecenis quotquot eunt dies,
amice, places illacrimabilem
    Plutona tauris, qui ter amplum
        Geryonen Tityonque tristi

How close the realm of dusky Proserpine
Yawned at that instant! I half glimpsed the dire
Judge of the dead, the blest in their divine
Seclusion, Sappho on the Aeolian lyre

Mourning the cold girls of her native isle,
And you, Alcaeus, more full-throatedly
Singing with your gold quill of ships, exile
And war, hardship on land, hardship at sea.

The admiring accord the reverent hush
Due to them both; but when the theme is war
And tyrants banished, then the elbowing crush
Thickens, the ghostly hearers thirst for more.

No wonder, when such music can disarm
The hundred-headed Hell-dog till he droops
His dark ears in bewilderment, can charm
The snakes that braid the Furies' hair in loops,

Yes, even beguile Prometheus and the sire
Of Pelops of their torments. Even Orion,
Leaving the chase to listen to the lyre,
Forgets the shy lynx or the shadowy lion.

14

Ah, how they glide by, Postumus, Postumus,
The years, the swift years! Wrinkles and imminent
　　Old age and death, whom no one conquers –
　　　　Piety cannot delay their onward

March; no, my friend, not were you to sacrifice
Three hundred bulls each day to inflexible
　　Pluto, whose grim moat holds the triple
　　　　Geryon jailed with his fellow Giants –

compescit unda, scilicet omnibus,
quicumque terrae munere vescimur,
    enaviganda, sive reges
        sive inopes erimus coloni.

frustra cruento Marte carebimus
fractisque rauci fluctibus Hadriae,
    frustra per autumnos nocentem
        corporibus metuemus Austrum:

visendus ater flumine languido
Cocytos errans et Danai genus
    infame damnatusque longi
        Sisyphus Aeolides laboris:

linquenda tellus et domus et placens
uxor, neque harum quas colis arborum
    te praeter invisas cupressos
        ulla brevem dominum sequetur:

absumet heres Caecuba dignior
servata centum clavibus et mero
    tinget pavimentum superbo,
        pontificum potiore cenis.

XV

Iam pauca aratro iugera regiae
moles relinquent, undique latius
    extenta visentur Lucrino
        stagna lacu, plantanusque caelebs

evincet ulmos; tum violaria et
myrtus et omnis copia narium
    spargent olivetis odorem
        fertilibus domino priori;

Death's lake that all we sons of mortality
Who have the good earth's fruits for the picking are
   Foredoomed to cross, no matter whether
     Rulers of kingdoms or needy peasants.

In vain we stay unscratched by the bloody wars,
In vain escape tumultuous Hadria's
   Storm-waves, in vain each autumn dread the
     Southern sirocco, our health's destroyer.

We must at last set eyes on the scenery
Of Hell: the ill-famed daughters of Danaus,
   Cocytus' dark, slow, winding current,
     Sisyphus damned to his endless labour.

Farewell to lands, home, dear and affectionate
Wife then. Of all those trees that you tended well
   Not one, a true friend, save the hated
     Cypress shall follow its short-lived master.

An heir shall drain those cellars of Caecuban
You treble-locked (indeed he deserves it more)
   And drench the stone-flagged floor with prouder
     Wine than is drunk at the pontiffs' banquet.

15

Soon I foresee few acres for harrowing
Left once the rich men's villas have seized the land;
   Fishponds that outdo Lake Lucrinus
     Everywhere; bachelor plane-trees ousting

Vine-loving elms; thick myrtle-woods, violet-beds,
All kinds of rare blooms tickling the sense of smell,
   Perfumes to drown those olive orchards
     Nursed in the past for a farmer's profit;

tum spissa ramis laurea fervidos
excludet ictus. non ita Romuli
   praescriptum et intonsi Catonis
     auspiciis veterumque norma.

privatus illis census erat brevis,
commune magnum: nulla decempedis
   metata privatis opacam
     porticus excipiebat Arcton,

nec fortuitum spernere caespitem
leges sinebant, oppida publico
   sumptu iubentes et deorum
     templa novo decorare saxo.

XVI

Otium divos rogat in patenti
prensus Aegaeo, simul atra nubes
condidit lunam neque certa fulgent
   sidera nautis;

otium bello furiosa Thrace,
otium Medi pharetra decori,
Grosphe, non gemmis neque purpura ve-
   nale neque auro.

non enim gazae neque consularis
summovet lictor miseros tumultus
mentis et curas laqueata circum
   tecta volantis.

vivitur parvo bene, cui paternum
splendet in mensa tenui salinum
nec levis somnos timor aut cupido
   sordidus aufert.

Quaint garden-screens, too, woven of laurel-boughs
To parry sunstroke. Romulus never urged
　This style of life; rough-bearded Cato
　　Would have detested the modern fashions.

Small private wealth, large communal property –
So ran the rule then. No one had porticoes
　Laid out with ten-foot builder's measures,
　　Trapping the cool of the northern shadow.

No one in those days sneered at the turf by the
Roadside; yet laws bade citizens beautify
　Townships at all men's cost and quarry
　　Glorious marble to roof the temples.

16

Peace and calm seas the voyager begs the gods for
When storms blow up in mid-Aegean, and black clouds
Muffle the moon, and sailors miss the usual
　Stars in the sky;

And peace is what the battle-maddened Thracians
And the fierce Parthians with their painted quivers
Pray for – the peace no gold or gems or purple,
　Grosphus, can buy.

A pasha's bribes, a consul's rodded lictors
Can soon disperse a riot of the people,
But not the grey mob of the mind, the worries
　Circling the beams

Of fretted ceilings. He lives well on little
Whose family salt-dish glitters on a plain-laid
Table; no fears or ugly longings steal his
　Innocent dreams.

quid brevi fortes iaculamur aevo
multa? quid terras alio calentis
sole mutamus? patriae quis exsul
　　se quoque fugit?

scandit aeratas vitiosa navis
Cura nec turmas equitum relinquit,
ocior cervis et agente nimbos
　　ocior Euro.

laetus in praesens animus quod ultra est
oderit curare et amara lento
temperet risu; nihil est ab omni
　　parte beatum.

abstulit clarum cita mors Achillem,
longa Tithonum minuit senectus,
et mihi forsan, tibi quod negarit,
　　porriget hora.

te greges centum Siculaeque circum
mugiunt vaccae, tibi tollit hinnitum
apta quadrigis equa, te bis Afro
　　murice tinctae

vestiunt lanae: mihi parva rura et
spiritum Graiae tenuem Camenae
Parca non mendax dedit et malignum
　　spernere vulgus.

XVII

Cur me querelis exanimas tuis?
nec dis amicum est nec mihi te prius
　　obire, Maecenas, mearum
　　　　grande decus columenque rerum.

Why do we aim so high, when time must foil our
Brave archery ? Why hanker after countries
Heated by foreign suns ? What exile ever
    Fled his own mind ?

Care, that contagion, clambers up the bronze-prowed
Galley, keeps level with the galloping squadron,
Outruns the stag and leaves the cloud-compelling
    East wind behind.

Happy with here and now, scorning hereafter,
Heart, with an easy humorousness attemper
The bitterness of things. Nothing is perfect
    Seen from all sides.

Death snatched away Achilles in his glory,
Long-drawn-out age wasted Tithonus inchmeal,
And any day may keep from you some blessing
    Which it provides

Me with. Sicilian cattle moo, a hundred
Herds, in your meadow, mares trained for the race-track
Neigh in your stalls, you dress in Tyrian purple,
    Double-dyed woof;

But I am rich too: Fate, an honest patron,
Has given me a small farm, an ear fine-tuned to
The Grecian Muses, and a mind from vulgar
    Envy aloof.

17

You kill me with your invalid worries. Why
These moans, Maecenas ? Both the gods and I
    Would be distressed if you, the great
    Glory and prop of my estate,

a! te meae si partem animae rapit
maturior vis, quid moror altera,
    nec carus aeque nec superstes
        integer ? ille dies utramque

ducet ruinam. non ego perfidum
dixi sacramentum: ibimus, ibimus,
    utcumque praecedes, supremum
        carpere iter comites parati.

me nec Chimaerae spiritus igneae
nec, si resurgat, centimanus Gyas
    divellet umquam: sic potenti
        Iustitiae placitumque Parcis.

seu Libra seu me Scorpios aspicit
formidulosus, pars violentior
    natalis horae, seu tyrannus
        Hesperiae Capricornus undae,

utrumque nostrum incredibili modo
consentit astrum: te Iovis impio
    tutela Saturno refulgens
        eripuit volucrisque Fati

tardavit alas, cum populus frequens
laetum theatris ter crepuit sonum:
    me truncus illapsus cerebro
        sustulerat, nisi Faunus ictum

dextra levasset, Mercurialium
custos virorum. reddere victimas
    aedemque votivam memento:
        nos humilem feriemus agnam.

Were to die first. If sickness wrenched away
Half of my soul, how could the robbed part stay
    Behind, a crippled fragment worth
    Far less? The same day shall heap earth

Over us both. I take the soldier's oath:
You lead, and we shall go together, both
    Ready to tread the road that ends
    All roads, inseparable friends.

Chimaera's fiery breath or, should he rise,
Gyas's hundred hands shall never prise
    Us two apart: iron Destiny
    And Justice on that score agree.

Whether the Scales looked down when I was born,
Or terrible Scorpio or Capricorn,
    Lord of the western seas, had power
    To dominate my natal hour,

Our stars are linked in marvellous unison.
Think back: malignant Saturn was outshone
    By Jupiter, your advocate,
    That time he rescued you – when Fate

Swooped but he stayed her wings, and in your cause
The glad, packed theatre crackled with applause
    Three times. And once a falling tree
    Was on the point of braining me

When Faunus, friend of poets, blocked the blow.
Our debts still stand. Remember that you owe
    A victim and a votive shrine:
    A humble lamb will settle mine.

XVIII

Non ebur neque aureum
mea renidet in domo lacunar,
 non trabes Hymettiae
premunt columnas ultima recisas
 Africa, neque Attali
ignotus heres regiam occupavi,
 nec Laconicas mihi
trahunt honestae purpuras clientae:
 at fides et ingeni
benigna vena est, pauperemque dives
 me petit: nihil supra
deos lacesso nec potentem amicum
 largiora flagito,
satis beatus unicis Sabinis.
 truditur dies die,
novaeque pergunt interire lunae:
 tu secanda marmora
locas sub ipsum funus et sepulcri
 immemor struis domos
marisque Bais obstrepentis urges
 summovere litora,
parum locuples continente ripe.
 quid quod usque proximos
revellis agri terminos et ultra
 limites clientium
salis avarus ? pellitur paternos
 in sinu ferens deos
et uxor et vir sordidosque natos.
 nulla certior tamen
rapacis Orci fine destinata
 aula divitem manet
erum. quid ultra tendis ? aequa tellus

18

No gold or ivory gleams
On panelled ceilings in my house; no marble beams
  Hewn on Hymettus press
Great columns quarried from the Libyan wilderness;
  No eastern millionaire
Ever made me his palace's unwitting heir;
  No well-born ladies dressed
In Spartan purple wait on me. Yet I am blessed
  With honesty and a streak
Of golden talent, and, though poor, rich people seek
  Me out. I do not task
The charity of the gods, nor from my patron ask
  Greater reward than this:
My one dear Sabine farm is wealth enough and bliss.
  Day dispossesses day,
Moons hurry to be born and race to their decay;
  Yet you, blind to the fact
Of imminent death, with one foot in the grave contract
  For marble to build more
Villas and, not content to own the mainland shore,
  Push out your property
From Baiae's beaches to displace the growling sea.
  Nor is that all. You rip
Marking-posts out of neighbours' fields and greedily skip
  Into your tenants' lands.
Next day they leave, their household gods clutched in their
    hands,
  Their ragged children held
Tight in their arms, a homeless man and wife, expelled.
  Be warned, though. No hall waits
More surely for its lord than the predestined gates
  Of greedy Death. Why toil
To add to your possessions? The impartial soil

   pauperi recluditur
regumque pueris, nec satelles Orci
   callidum Promethea
revexit auro captus. hic superbum
   Tantalum atque Tantali
genus coercet, hic levare functum
   pauperem laboribus
vocatus atque non vocatus audit.

XIX

Bacchum in remotis carmina rupibus
vidi docentem – credite posteri –
   Nymphasque discentis et auris
     capripedum Satyrorum acutas.

Euhoe, recenti mens trepidat metu
plenoque Bacchi pectore turbidum
   laetatur: Euhoe, parce Liber,
     parce gravi metuende thyrso!

fas pervicaces est mihi Thyiadas
vinique fontem lactis et uberes
   cantare rivos atque truncis
     lapsa cavis iterare mella:

fas et beatae coniugis additum
stellis honorem tectaque Penthei
   disiecta non leni ruina
     Thracis et exitium Lycurgi.

tu flectis amnis, tu mare barbarum,
tu separatis uvidus in iugis
   nodo coerces viperino
     Bistonidum sine fraude crinis:

Opens herself to take
The pauper and the prince alike. No bribe could make
   Hell's ferryman alter course
To row clever Prometheus back. Death holds by force
   Proud Tantalus and the clan
Of Tantalus. He, when work is done and the poor man
   Begs him to ease his lot,
Comes to the call; indeed he comes, called for or not.

19

    I saw Bacchus today:
    In a wild gorge he lay,
Teaching his sacred melodies. O years
    To come, credit my glimpse
    Of the attentive nymphs
And goat-foot satyrs cocking pointed ears.

    Ai, ai, my mind still reels
    With the sharp dread, and feels
Tumultuous rapture, bursting with the god.
    Ai, ai, spare me, be kind,
    Unchainer of the mind,
Stern master of the fearful ivy-rod.

    Now I may celebrate
    Your tireless, unsedate
Revellers, your wine-fountains and the rich
    Runnels of milk that spring
    At your command. I sing
The honey dripping from the tree-trunk niche,

    I sing your radiant bride
    Who, crowned and glorified,
Among the constellations has her place,

tu, cum parentis regna per arduum
cohors Gigantum scanderet impia,
    Rhoetum retorsisti leonis
      unguibus horribilique mala;

quamquam choreis aptior et iocis
ludoque dictus non sat idoneus
    pugnae ferebaris: sed idem
      pacis eras mediusque belli.

te vidit insons Cerberus aureo
cornu decorum leniter atterens
    caudam et recedentis trilingui
      ore pedes tetigitque crura.

XX

Non usitata nec tenui ferar
penna biformis per liquidum aethera
    vates, neque in terris morabor
      longius, invidiaque maior

The palace roof razed flat
  At Thebes – no light stroke, that –
And King Lycurgus' grim demise in Thrace.

  You can divert the motion
  Of rivers, tame the ocean,
And, flushed with wine, upon some secret height,
  Bind the unruly curls
  Of the Bistonian girls
With knots of vipers impotent to bite.

  When the brigade of Giants
  In impious defiance
Of the steep sky broke the great Father's laws,
  You were the one who hurled
  Rhoetus to the underworld,
Donning the lion's terrible teeth and claws.

  Ready to dance and play
  And joke, but in the fray
Out of your element – so others thought;
  Nevertheless, you bore
  Yourself in peace and war
Equally well and in the thickest fought.

  Even Cerberus, when he spied
  You coming in the pride
Of godhead with your gold horn, gently swung
  His tail to wish you well
  And, as you passed through Hell,
Fawned on your ankles with his triple tongue.

20

Mine are no weak or borrowed wings: they'll bear
Me, bard made bird, through the compliant air,
Earthbound no longer, leaving far behind
The cities and the envy of mankind.

urbis relinquam. non ego pauperum
sanguis parentum, non ego quem vocas,
　dilecte Maecenas, obibo
　　nec Stygia cohibebor unda.

iam iam residunt cruribus asperae
pelles, et album mutor in alitem
　superne, nascunturque leves
　　per digitos umerosque plumae.

iam Daedaleo notior Icaro
visam gementis litora Bosphori
　Syrtisque Gaetulas canorus
　　ales Hyperboreosque campos.

me Colchus et qui dissimulat metum
Marsae cohortis Dacus et ultimi
　noscent Geloni, me peritus
　　discet Hiber Rhodanique potor.

absint inani funere neniae
luctusque turpes et querimoniae;
　compesce clamorem ac sepulcri
　　mitte supervacuos honores.

Dearest Maecenas, I who was the child
Of a poor family, I who have been styled
Your shadow, need not as a shadow lie
Cramped by the Styx, nor die as others die.
Already the rough skin is forming on
My ankles; metamorphosis into swan
Moves up my body; downy plumage springs
On arms and elbows; shoulder-blades sprout wings.
And now I rise, singing, a portent more
Talked of than Icarus was, ready to soar
Over the roaring Bosphorus, the quicksands
Of Syrtes and the Hyperborean lands.
In Colchis and in Dacia, where they feign
Scorn of our Marsian troops, in ignorant Spain,
In farthest Thrace my verses shall be known:
Gauls shall drink Horace as they do the Rhone.
No dirges, please. Mine being no real death,
Tears would be ugly, sighs a waste of breath.
Restrain your noisy sorrow, then, and save
Yourself the needless rituals of the grave.

Q
HORATI
FLACCI
CARMINUM
LIBER TERTIUS

THE ODES OF
HORACE
BOOK
THREE

I

Odi profanum vulgus et arceo;
favete linguis: carmina non prius
   audita Musarum sacerdos
    virginibus puerisque canto.

regum timendorum in proprios greges,
reges in ipsos imperium est Iovis,
   clari Giganteo triumpho,
    cuncta supercilio moventis.

est ut viro vir latius ordinet
arbusta sulcis, hic generosior
   descendat in Campum petitor,
    moribus hic meliorque fama

contendat, illi turba clientium
sit maior: aequa lege Necessitas
   sortitur insignis et imos;
    onne capax movet urna nomen.

destrictus ensis cui super impia
cervice pendet, non Siculae dapes
   dulcem elaborabunt saporem,
    non avium citharaeque cantus

somnum reducent: somnus agrestium
lenis virorum non humilis domos
   fastidit umbrosamque ripam,
    non Zephyris agitata Tempe.

desiderantem quod satis est neque
tumultuosum sollicitat mare
   nec saevus Arcturi cadentis
    impetus aut orientis Haedi,

1

I have no use for secular outsiders,
I bar the gross crowd. Give me reverent silence.
   I am the Muses' priest:
I sing for maidens and for boys grave verse

Unheard before. Earth's kings may awe their own flocks,
But kings themselves are under Jove, the glorious
   Conqueror of the Giants,
Who with an eyebrow moves the universe.

One man plants vineyards broader than his neighbour's.
To the Field of Mars three candidates for office
   Descend: one hopes high birth
Will gain the day, another purer fame

And character, the third his mob of clients.
Yet still Necessity, the same just dealer,
   Allots to high and low
Their fates: her large urn shuffles every name.

When the bare sword-blade hangs over a villain's
Neck, the elaborate Syracusan banquet
   Loses its savour; then
No sound of lyres or birds in aviaries

Will bring him sleep again – sweet sleep that's never
Too proud to visit the poor peasant's cottage,
   A shady river-bank,
Or any valley ruffled by a breeze.

The sea's disturbances cannot disturb his
Spirit who covets only what is needful,
   Nor the fierce squalls that pounce
When the Kid rises or Arcturus wanes,

non verberatae grandine vineae
fundusque mendax, arbore nunc aquas
    culpante, nunc torrentia agros
        sidera, nunc hiemes iniquas.

contracta pisces aequora sentiunt
iactis in altum molibus; huc frequens
    caementa demittit redemptor
        cum famulis dominusque terrae

fastidiosus: sed Timor et Minae
scandunt eodem quo dominus, neque
    decedit aerata triremi et
        post equitem sedet atra Cura.

quodsi dolentem nec Phrygius lapis
nec purpurarum sidere clarior
    delenit usus nec Falerna
        vitis Achaemeniumque costum,

cur invidendis postibus et novo
sublime ritu moliar atrium ?
    cur valle permutem Sabina
        divitias operosiores ?

II

Angustam amice pauperiem pati
robustus acri militia puer
    condiscat et Parthos feroces
        vexet eques metuendus hasta

vitamque sub divo et trepidis agat
in rebus. illum ex moenibus hosticis
    matrona bellantis tyranni
        prospiciens et adulta virgo

Nor hail that batters vineyards flat, nor orchards
That break their promise and lay all the blame on
   The stars that scorch the fields
Or mischief-making winter or the rains.

Look where the builder with his horde of navvies
Drives the stone pilings deep into the water
   (The cramped fish lose more sea)
And tips in rubble for the millionaire

Bored with dry land. But Fear and the Forebodings
Can climb as many storeys as the owner.
   There on the bronze-beaked yacht
Or perched behind the horseman squats black Care.

Will purple silks more lustrous than the starlight
Or mottled Phrygian marble allay sorrow?
   Can the Falernian vine
Or nard from Persia remedy ill health?

Then why should I take pains to build a high hall
In the new style with doors to welcome envy?
   Why change my Sabine vale
For the large inconvenience of wealth?

2

Disciplined in the school of hard campaigning,
Let the young Roman study how to bear
Rigorous difficulties without complaining,
And camp with danger in the open air,

And with his horse and lance become the scourge of
Wild Parthians. From the ramparts of the town
Of the warring king, the princess on the verge of
Womanhood with her mother shall look down

suspiret, eheu, ne rudis agminum
sponsus lacessat regius asperum
   tactu leonem, quem cruenta
     per medias rapit ira caedis.

dulce et decorum est pro patria mori:
mors et fugacem persequitur virum,
   nec parcit imbellis iuventae
     poplitibus timidove tergo.

Virtus repulsae nescia sordidae
intaminatis fulget honoribus,
   nec sumit aut ponit securis
     arbitrio popularis aurae.

Virtus, recludens immeritis mori
caelum, negata temptat iter via,
   coetusque vulgaris et udam
     spernit humum fugiente penna.

est et fideli tuta silentio
merces: vetabo, qui Cereris sacrum
   vulgarit arcanae, sub isdem
     sit trabibus fragilemque mecum

solvat phaselon: saepe Diespiter
neglectus incesto addidit integrum:
   raro antecedentem scelestum
     deseruit pede Poena claudo.

III

Iustum et tenacem propositi virum
non civium ardor prava iubentium,
   non vultus instantis tyranni
     mente quatit solida neque Auster,

And sigh, 'Ah, royal lover, still a stranger
To battle, do not recklessly excite
That lion, savage to touch, whom murderous anger
Drives headlong through the thickest of the fight.'

The glorious and the decent way of dying
Is for one's country. Run, and death will seize
You no less surely. The young coward, flying,
Gets his quietus in the back and knees.

Unconscious of mere loss of votes and shining
With honours that the mob's breath cannot dim,
True worth is not found raising or resigning
The fasces at the wind of popular whim.

To those who do not merit death, exploring
Ways barred to ordinary men, true worth
Opens a path to heaven and spurns on soaring
Pinions the trite crowds and the clogging earth.

Trusty discretion too shall be rewarded
Duly. I will not suffer a tell-tale
Of Ceres' sacred mysteries to be boarded
Under my roof or let my frail boat sail

With him; for, slighted, often God confuses
The innocent with the evil-doer's fate.
Yet Vengeance, with one lame foot, seldom loses
Track of the outlaw, though she sets off late.

3

A mob of citizens clamouring for injustice,
An autocrat's grimace of rage, the south wind,
    That moody emperor
Of the wild Adriatic, even the hand

dux inquieti turbidus Hadriae,
nec fulminantis magna manus Iovis:
   si fractus illabatur orbis,
     impavidum ferient ruinae.

hac arte Pollux et vagus Hercules
enisus arces attigit igneas,
   quos inter Augustus recumbens
     purpureo bibet ore nectar.

hac te merentem, Bacche pater, tuae
vexere tigres indocili iugum
   collo trahentes; hac Quirinus
     Martis equis Acheronta fugit,

gratum elocuta consiliantibus
Iunone divis: 'Ilion, Ilion
   fatalis incestusque iudex
     et mulier peregrina vertit

in pulverem, ex quo destituit deos
mercede pacta Laomedon, mihi
   castaeque damnatum Minervae
     cum populo et duce fraudulento.

iam nec Lacaenae splendet adulterae
famosus hospes nec Priami domus
   periura pugnaces Achivos
     Hectoreis opibus refringit,

nostrisque ductum seditionibus
bellum resedit. protinus et gravis
   iras et invisum nepotem,
     Troica quem peperit sacerdos,

Marti redonabo; illum ego lucidas
inire sedes, discere nectaris
   sucos et adscribi quietis
     ordinibus patiar deorum.

Of Jove who grips the thunder cannot stagger
The just and steady-purposed man. His mind is
  Rock. If the heavens crack
And fall, he'll coolly let the ruin rain.

By this same quality the wandering Hercules
And Pollux stormed the starry ramparts (with them
  Augustus before long
Shall lie and sip the nectar, ruddy-mouthed).

Such courage, Father Bacchus, earned you glory
When, docile-necked, the harnessed tigers drew you
  Westwards. And Romulus,
Who fled from death behind the steeds of Mars,

By that brave action swayed the gods in council
When Juno spoke this welcome: 'Ilium, Ilium,
  A fatal arbiter
Who chose corruptly and a foreign whore

Have turned you into dust: people and paltering
Monarch became my forfeit and the virgin
  Minerva's – doomed the day
Laomedon robbed the gods of payment due.

That worst of guests, the Spartan woman's strutting
Hero, is dead; Hector can bring no help now;
  The house of Priam broke
Its promises, and now the doughty Greeks

Have broken it. The long war, which our quarrels
Made longer still, fades to a whisper. Mars, take
  Your Trojan priestess' child,
My hated grandson. With him I resign

My unrelenting grudge. Let Romulus enter
Our lucent regions, learn the taste of nectar
  And be enrolled with us
In the serene society of gods.

dum longus inter saeviat Ilion
Romamque pontus, qualibet exsules
   in parte regnanto beati;
      dum Priami Paridisque busto

insultet armentum et catulos ferae
celent inultae, stet Capitolium
   fulgens triumphatisque possit
      Roma ferox dare iura Medis.

horrenda late nomen in ultimas
extendat oras, qua medius liquor
   secernit Europen ab Afro,
      qua tumidus rigat arva Nilus,

aurum irrepertum et sic melius situm,
cum terra celat, spernere fortior
   quam cogere humanos in usus
      omne sacrum rapiente dextra.

quicumque mundo terminus obstitit,
hunc tanget armis, visere gestiens,
   qua parte debacchentur ignes,
      qua nebulae pluviique rores.

sed bellicosis fata Quiritibus
hac lege dico, ne nimium pii
   rebusque fidentes avitae
      tecta velint reparare Troiae.

Troiae renascens alite lugubri
fortuna tristi clade iterabitur,
   ducente victrices catervas
      coniuge me Iovis et sorore.

ter si resurgat murus aeneus
auctore Phoebo, ter pereat meis
   excisus Argivis, ter uxor
      capta virum puerosque ploret.'

While the broad sea parts Troy and Rome, still raging
Between them, let the refugees be happy
   Ruling whát land they please;
As long as cattle trample on the tomb

Of Paris and King Priam and the wild beasts
Hide their whelps safely there, let the great Capitol
   Glitter foursquare and Rome,
The soldier-queen, teach subject Medes the law,

Spreading her name and terror to the limits
Of east and west, from where the mid-sea severs
   Europe from Africa
To where the gross Nile drenches Egypt's soil.

To run away with scorn from undiscovered
Gold (better left where the earth conceals it) rather
   Than force it to man's use
With snatching, sacrilegious hands – there lies

Her destined source of power. Legions shall push to
The world's fixed ends, eager to see the sights there,
   The frenzied dance of heat
And the cold revelries of mist and storm.

This fortune I foretell for the fierce Romans,
But on these terms: that no fanatic piety
   Or overconfidence
Lead them to re-roof their ancestral home.

Should Troy revive, omens of doom shall dog her
And bitter ruin be renewed. I, sister
   And wife of Jove, myself
Shall head the conquering regiments again.

If Phoebus lets the bronze wall rise a third time,
It shall be levelled by my Greeks a third time,
   And the young captive wife
Shall once more mourn her husband and her sons.'

non hoc iocosae conveniet lyrae:
quo, Musa, tendis? desine pervicax
   referre sermones deorum et
      magna modis tenuare parvis.

IV

Descende caelo et dic age tibia
regina longum Calliope melos,
   seu voce nunc mavis acuta,
      seu fidibus citharave Phoebi.

auditis an me ludit amabilis
insania? audire et videor pios
   errare per lucos, amoenae
      quos et aquae subeunt et aurae.

me fabulosae Vulture in avio
nutricis extra limen Apuliae
   ludo fatigatumque somno
      fronde nova puerum palumbes

texere, mirum quod foret omnibus
quicumque celsae nidum Acherontiae
   saltusque Bantinos et arvum
      pingue tenent humilis Forenti,

ut tuto ab atris corpore viperis
dormirem et ursis, ut premerer sacra
   lauroque collataque myrto,
      non sine dis animosus infans.

vester, Camenae, vester in arduos
tollor Sabinos, seu mihi frigidum
   Praeneste seu Tibur supinum
      seu liquidae placuere Baiae.

Where are you rambling, Muse? This theme's beyond your
Light-hearted lyre. End now. Absurd presumption
  To tell tales of the gods
And mar high matters with your reedy voice!

4

Descend, divine Calliope, from heaven
And play a long, a solemn song, with flute as
  Accompaniment or else
Apollo's lyre, or sing, clear-voiced, alone.

Listen! Or is it kind hallucination
Deceiving me? I seem to glimpse her music,
  I roam through hallowed groves
Where pleasant winds and waters wander too.

Signs marked my boyhood. Once, on pathless Vultur,
Beyond the borders of my nurse Apulia,
  Play-worn and sleep-inclined
I lay down and the legendary doves

Wove me a blanket of the leaves just fallen.
In Bantia's glades, high in the village-eyrie
  Of Acherontia
And through Forentum's fertile valleys, folk

Marvelled at how the bears and black snakes left me
Tucked in my coverlet of bay and myrtle
  To sleep on, safe, a babe
And unafraid, watched over by the gods.

Whether I climb my own steep slopes or pass time
In hill-perched Tibur or cool-aired Praeneste
  Or Baiae's cloudless bay,
Dear Muses, I am yours, fatefully yours.

vestris amicum fontibus et choris
non me Philippis versa acies retro,
    devota non exstinxit arbos,
        nec Sicula Palinurus unda.

utcumque mecum vos eritis, libens
insanientem navita Bosphorum
    temptabo et urentis harenas
        litoris Assyrii viator,

visam Britannos hospitibus feros
et laetum equino sanguine Concanum,
    visam pharetratos Gelonos
        et Scythicum inviolatus amnem.

vos Caesarem altum, militia simul
fessas cohortis abdidit oppidis,
    finire quaerentem labores
        Pierio recreatis antro.

vos lene consilium et datis et dato
gaudetis almae. scimus ut impios
    Titanas immanemque turbam
        fulmine sustulerit caduco,

qui terram inertem, qui mare temperat
ventosum, et urbes regnaque tristia
    divosque mortalisque turmas
        imperio regi unus aequo.

magnum illa terrorem intulerat Iovi
fidens iuventus horrida bracchiis
    fratresque tendentes opaco
        Pelion imposuisse Olympo.

sed quid Typhoeus et validus Mimas,
aut quid minaci Porphyrion statu,
    quid Rhoetus evulsisque truncis
        Enceladus iaculator audax

Because I love your fountains and your dances,
You saved me when the ranks broke at Philippi,
   And when that cursed tree tried
To murder me, and when the sea ran high

Off Palinurus' cape. With you beside me
I'll undertake great explorations, gladly
   Sail the wild Bosphorus, cross
The torrid deserts of the Persian Gulf,

Travel among the stranger-hating Britons,
See quivered Scythians camping on the Don's banks,
   Or Concani who gulp
The blood of horses, and return unharmed.

When he has hidden his war-weary cohorts
Among the towns, who gives great Caesar solace
   In the Pierian cave
And longed-for rest from government but you,

Kind ones, who prompt us gently and rejoice in
The wisdom we accept? We know the story
   Of how He who controls
The brute earth and the wind-stirred sea and rules,

Just and supreme, the cities of the living,
The sad realm of the dead and all immortal
   And mortal gatherings,
Felled the massed impious Titans with his flung

Thunderbolt when that young crew raised defiant
Fists and the brothers piled pine-dark Olympus
   On Pelion and built
Mutiny to the height of Jove's dismay.

Yet how could mighty Mimas or Typhoeus
Or Rhoetus or Porphyrion for all his
   Colossal rage or fierce
Enceladus who tore up trees for darts

contra sonantem Palladis aegida
possent ruentes ? hinc avidus stetit
   Vulcanus, hinc matrona Iuno et
      numquam umeris positurus arcum,

qui rore puro Castaliae lavit
crinis solutos, qui Lyciae tenet
   dumeta natalemque silvam,
      Delius et Patareus Apollo.

vis consili expers mole ruit sua:
vim temperatam di quoque provehunt
   in maius; idem odere viris
      omne nefas animo moventis.

testis mearum centimanus Gyas
sententiarum, notus et integrae
   temptator Orion Dianae,
      virginea domitus sagitta.

iniecta monstris Terra dolet suis
maeretque partus fulmine luridum
   missos ad Orcum; nec peredit
      impositam celer ignis Aetnen,

incontinentis nec Tityi iecur
reliquit ales, nequitiae additus
   custos; amatorem trecentae
      Pirithoum cohibent catenae.

V

Caelo tonantem credidimus Iovem
regnare: praesens divus habebitur
   Augustus adiectis Britannis
      imperio gravibusque Persis.

Succeed? Their charge wilted against the ringing
Shield of Athene. Battle-hungry Vulcan
   Stood by, Queen Juno too,
And he who never leaves his arm bow-bare,

Who bathes his loose hair in the pure Castalian
Fountain – Apollo, lord of Lycia's thickets,
   Guardian of Patara
And Delos, where his native woodlands are.

Primitive force topples to its own ruin,
But when the mind guides power it prospers; heaven
   Helps it: the gods abhor
Brute strength devoted to malignant ends.

Gyas the hundred-handed and Orion,
Who laid hands on inviolable Diana
   And died by her chaste shaft,
Bear witness to the truth I have set down.

Earth, heaped over her monsters, groans and curses
The bolt that hurled them into pallid Hades;
   The Giant that Etna pins
Still spouts up fire to eat away his tomb;

Even now the vulture, lust's appointed jailer,
Tears at the liver of incontinent Tityos;
   Hundreds of chains still bind
Pirithous whose passion broke the law.

5

Thunder in heaven confirms our faith – Jove rules there;
But here on earth Augustus shall be hailed as
   God also, when he makes
New subjects of the Briton and the dour

milesne Crassi coniuge barbara
turpis maritus vixit et hostium –
    pro curia inversique mores! –
      consenuit socerorum in armis

sub rege Medo Marsus et Apulus,
anciliorum et nominis et togae
    oblitus aeternaeque Vestae,
      incolumi Iove et urbe Roma?

hoc caverat mens provida Reguli
dissentientis condicionibus
    foedis et exemplo trahenti
      perniciem veniens in aevum,

si non periret immiserabilis
captiva pubes. 'signa ego Punicis
    adfixa delubris et arma
      militibus sine caede' dixit

'derepta vidi; vidi ego civium
retorta tergo bracchia libero
    portasque non clausas et arva
      Marte coli populata nostro.

auro repensus scilicet acrior
miles redibit. flagitio additis
    damnum: neque amissos colores
      lana refert medicata fuco,

nec vera virtus, cum semel excidit,
curat reponi deterioribus.
    si pugnat extricata densis
      cera plagis, erit ille fortis

qui perfidis se credidit hostibus,
et Marte Poenos proteret altero,
    qui lora restrictis lacertis
      sensit iners timuitque mortem.

Parthian. Did Crassus' troops live in dishonour
With Medish wives and grow grey-headed serving
  (O Roman Senate! O
Custom corrupted!) a barbarian power

And enemy in-laws? Marsians, Apulians,
Forget the Sacred Shields, Rome's name, the toga
  And Vesta's deathless flame,
While Jupiter's temple and the City stood

Unharmed? This was the shame far-seeing Regulus
Guarded against when he refused a base peace
  And spurned the precedent
That would have brought the unborn age no good:

And so the captives forfeited his pity,
The young men died. 'For I have seen our eagles
  Nailed to the Punic shrines,'
Regulus said, 'swords wrested from our men

And no blood spilt; with these eyes I have witnessed
The hands of citizens and free men pinioned
  Behind their backs, the gates
Of Carthage wide, their scarred fields tilled again.

As if a soldier hurried back to battle
Fiercer for being ransomed! Sirs, you are heaping
  Loss upon shame. When wool
Is dipped in purple, farewell to its white

Purity. Courage, likewise, once departed,
Is slow to pay failed hearts a second visit.
  If does, freed from the net,
Make no resistance, will a man show fight

Who gave himself to known perfidious enemies?
Will he take arms again to wear down Carthage
  Who meekly let his wrists
Feel ropes and would not look death in the face?

hic, unde vitam sumeret inscius,
pacem duello miscuit. o pudor!
  o magna Carthago, probrosis
   altior Italiae ruinis!'

fertur pudicae coniugis osculum
parvosque natos ut capitis minor
  ab se removisse et virilem
   torvus humi posuisse vultum,

donec labantis consilio patres
firmaret auctor numquam alias dato,
  interque maerentis amicos
   egregius properaret exsul.

atqui sciebat quae sibi barbarus
tortor pararet; non aliter tamen
  dimovit obstantis propinquos
   et populum reditus morantem

quam si clientum longa negotia
diiudicata lite relinqueret,
  tendens Venafranos in agros
   aut Lacedaemonium Tarentum.

VI

Delicta maiorum immeritus lues,
Romane, donec templa refeceris
  aedesque labentis deorum et
   foeda nigro simulacra fumo.

dis te minorem quod geris, imperas:
hinc omne principium, huc refer exitum:
  di multa neglecti dederunt
   Hesperiae mala luctuosae.

Blind to his source of safety, he confuses
The qualities of peace and war. Thus honour
   Dies and great Carthage climbs
Higher on Italy's ruin and disgrace!'

They say he drew back from the kiss his true wife
And little children begged, and like a prisoner
   Deprived of civil rights
Bent an austere gaze grimly on the ground,

Until his unexampled admonition
Had fixed the wavering Senate in their purpose
   And he could push through crowds
Of grieving friends, exile- and glory-bound.

And yet he knew what the barbarian torturer
Had ready for him. Kinsmen blocked his passage,
   The people held him back,
But he returned as unconcernedly

As if they were his clients and he'd settled
Some lengthy lawsuit for them and was going
   On to Venafrum's fields
Or to Tarentum, Sparta's colony.

6

Roman, you may be innocent of guilt,
Yet you shall pay for each ancestral crime,
Until our mouldering temples are rebuilt
And the gods' statues cleansed of smoke and grime.

Only as servant of the gods in heaven
Can you rule earth. The seed of action is
Theirs, and the fruit. Slighted, have they not given
Suffering Italy multiple miseries?

iam bis Monaeses et Pacori manus
non auspicatos contudit impetus
   nostros et adiecisse praedam
     torquibus exiguis renidet.

paene occupatam seditionibus
delevit urbem Dacus et Aethiops,
   hic classe formidatus, ille
     missilibus melior sagittis.

fecunda culpae saecula nuptias
primum inquinavere et genus et domos;
   hoc fonte derivata clades
     in patriam populumque fluxit.

motus doceri gaudet Ionicos
matura virgo et fingitur artibus
   iam nunc et incestos amores
     de tenero meditatur ungui;

mox iuniores quaerit adulteros
inter mariti vina, neque eligit
   cui donet impermissa raptim
     gaudia luminibus remotis,

sed iussa coram non sine conscio
surgit marito, seu vocat institor
   seu navis Hispanae magister,
     dedecorum pretiosus emptor.

non his iuventus orta parentibus
infecit aequor sanguine Punico,
   Pyrrhumque et ingentem cecidit
     Antiochum Hannibalemque dirum,

sed rusticorum mascula militum
proles, Sabellis docta ligonibus
   versare glebas et severae
     matris ad arbitrium recisos

Pacorus and Monaeses have now twice
Bruised our ill-starred assaults. Loot from our tents
Has made them jubilant and enhanced the price
Of their poor necklaces and ornaments.

And, ridden by civil faction, Rome came near
To her annihilation and eclipse
When Dacia, linked with Egypt, made us fear
Her archers as we did her ally's ships.

This age has proved fertile in evil. First
It stained the marriage vow, and then the home,
And thence pure blood; and from this fouled source burst
The river of ruin that has flooded Rome.

Watch the grown girl. She revels in being taught
Dances from Asia Minor; she perfects
The arts of provocation; her one thought
From top to tingling toe is lawless sex.

Soon she's pursuing young philanderers
Among her husband's guests. Careless of whom
She chooses, hugger-mugger she confers
The illicit pleasure in a half-lit room.

Only the husband seeming not to note,
At any man's command she leaves her place,
Pedlar or captain of some Spanish boat –
Whoever pays the price of her disgrace.

Pyrrhus, Antiochus, Hannibal – the young
Romans who brought such enemies to their knees
And dyed the sea with Punic blood, were sprung
From parents of a different mould from these.

They were a hardy generation, good
Farmers and warriors, brought up to turn
The Sabine furrows with their hoes, chop wood
And lug the faggots home to please a stern

portare fustis, sol ubi montium
mutaret umbras et iuga demeret
    bobus fatigatis, amicum
        tempus agens abeunte curru.

damnosa quid non imminuit dies?
aetas parentum peior avis tulit
    nos nequiores, mox daturos
        progeniem vitiosiorem.

VII

Quid fles, Asterie, quem tibi candidi
primo restituent vere Favonii
    Thyna merce beatum,
        constantis iuvenem fide

Gygen? ille Notis actus ad Oricum
post insana Caprae sidera frigidas
    noctes non sine multis
        insomnis lacrimis agit.

atqui sollicitae nuntius hospitae,
suspirare Chloen et miseram tuis
    dicens ignibus uri,
        temptat mille vafer modis.

ut Proetum mulier perfida credulum
falsis impulerit criminibus nimis
    casto Bellerophontae
        maturare necem refert:

narrat paene datum Pelea Tartaro,
Magnessam Hippolyten dum fugit abstinens;
    et peccare docentis
        fallax historias monet.

Mother at evening when the sun relieves
The tired ox of the yoke and draws the shift-
ing shadows down the mountainside and leaves
The pleasant darkness as his parting gift.

Time corrupts all. What has it not made worse?
Our grandfathers sired feeble children; theirs
Were weaker still – ourselves; and now our curse
Must be to breed even more degenerate heirs.

7

Asterie, why these tears? For early spring
And the fair-weather breezes will soon bring
   Back from Bithynia, still true
   And rich with merchant revenue,

Your Gyges. Meanwhile the tempestuous Goat
And the south winds have buffeted his boat
   To Oricus, and there he keeps
   Awake through each cold night and weeps.

His love-sick hostess sends her maid to say
Poor Chloe's heaving sighs, smouldering away
   With fires as hot as yours. She uses
   A thousand cunning tempter's ruses.

Bellerophon, she argues, risked his life
Through being too pure for Proetus' faithless wife
   Who drove her husband to resort
   To murder by her false report.

High-minded Peleus who refused to bed
Hippolyte was nearly packed off dead
   To Tartarus. Thus she brings in
   Sly fables recommending sin –

frustra: nam scopulis surdior Icari
voces audit adhuc integer. at tibi
    ne vicinus Enipeus
        plus iusto placeat cave;

quamvis non alius flectere equum sciens
aeque conspicitur gramine Martio,
    nec quisquam citus aeque
        Tusco denatat alveo.

prima nocte domum claude neque in vias
sub cantu querulae despice tibiae,
    et te saepe vocanti
        duram difficilis mane.

VIII

Martiis caelebs quid agam Kalendis,
quid velint flores et acerra turis
plena miraris positusque carbo in
    caespite vivo,

docte sermones utriusque linguae?
voveram dulcis epulas et album
Libero caprum prope funeratus
    arboris ictu.

hic dies anno redeunte festus
corticem adstrictum pice dimovebit
amphorae fumum bibere institutae
    consule Tullo.

sume, Maecenas, cyathos amici
sospitis centum et vigiles lucernas
perfer in lucem: procul omnis esto
    clamor et ira.

In vain, for to that voice Gyges has proved
Deaf as the rocks of Icaros and unmoved.
  Look nearer home, girl, lest next door
  Young Enipeus attracts you more

Than decency allows (who, though, can match
Him riding on the Field of Mars and catch
  So many eyes? What rival swim
  Down Tiber and keep up with him?).

Lock up your doors at nightfall; do not crane
Into the street at his flute's wheedling strain;
  And, though he calls you hard of heart
  Day in, day out, stick to the part.

8

What is a bachelor doing on Matrons' Day,
The first of March? What can it mean – this cask
Of incense and these flowers? Why do I lay
Live embers on the fresh-cut turf? you ask,

You, the keen scholar and antiquary
In both tongues. Well, I vowed a tasty spread
And a white goat to Bacchus when that tree
Came down last year and almost stretched me dead;

And now this anniversary day shall rip
The cork from the wine-jar that was sealed with pitch
Back in the time of Tullus' consulship
And taught to drink smoke in the upstairs niche.

A hundred cupfuls, then, to toast your friend's
Deliverance, Maecenas, and till day
Breaks let the candles burn bright at both ends,
And argument and hubbub keep away!

mitte civilis super urbe curas:
occidit Daci Cotisonis agmen,
Medus infestus sibi luctuosis
   dissidet armis,

servit Hispanae vetus hostis orae
Cantaber sera domitus catena,
iam Scythae laxo meditantur arcu
   cedere campis.

neglegens ne qua populus laboret
parce privatus nimium cavere et
dona praesentis cape laetus horae ac
   linque severa.

IX

 'Donec gratus eram tibi
nec quisquam potior bracchia candidae
   cervici iuvenis dabat,
Persarum vigui rege beatior.'

 'donec non alia magis
arsisti neque erat Lydia post Chloen,
   multi Lydia nominis
Romana vigui clarior Ilia.'

 'me nunc Thressa Chloe regit,
dulcis docta modos et citharae sciens,
   pro qua non metuam mori,
si parcent animae fata superstiti.'

 'me torret face mutua
Thurini Calais filius Ornyti,
   pro quo bis patiar mori,
si parcent puero fata superstiti.'

Forget the cares of state and office. Chief
Cotiso is dead with all his Dacian host;
The dangerous Mede has come to civil grief,
His own worst enemy now; upon the coast

Of Spain the Cantaber, Rome's ancient foe,
Quelled and obedient, wears at last our chains;
Even the Scythian, with a slackened bow,
Is pondering withdrawal from his plains.

Be a plain citizen for once – you fret
Too much about the people's sufferings.
Relax. Take what the hour gives, gladly. Let
Others attend the graver side of things.

9

'When you loved me, dear Lydia, when
I was preferred and your white neck was
Not for the arms of other men,
I was as happy as the King of Persia then.'

'When you loved me, dear, when I came
First in your heart and Chloe second,
Then Lydia proudly wrote her name
Next to our Roman Ilia's in the roll of fame.'

'Chloe's queen now, my girl from Thrace,
Who sings and plays the lyre divinely.
If Fate would spare that darling face,
I'd suffer death unflinchingly in Chloe's place.'

'Ornytus' son from Thurii
Has fired my heart, and his is burning.
If Fate let him live and doomed me,
I'd die for Calais twice over willingly.'

'quid si prisca redit Venus
diductosque iugo cogit aeneo,
    si flava excutitur Chloe
reiectaeque patet ianua Lydiae?

'quamquam sidere pulchrior
ille est, tu levior cortice et improbo
    iracundior Hadria,
tecum vivere amem, tecum obeam libens.'

X

Extremum Tanain si biberes, Lyce,
saevo nupta viro, me tamen asperas
porrectum ante foris obicere incolis
    plorares Aquilonibus.

audis quo strepitu ianua, quo nemus
inter pulchra satum tecta remugiat
ventis, et positas ut glaciet nives
    puro numine Iuppiter?

ingratam Veneri pone superbiam,
ne currente retro funis eat rota.
non te Penelopen difficilem procis
    Tyrrhenus genuit parens.

o quamvis neque te munera nec preces
nec tinctus viola pallor amantium
nec vir Pieria paelice saucius
    curvat, supplicibus tuis

parcas, nec rigida mollior aesculo
nec Mauris animum mitior anguibus.
non hoc semper erit liminis aut aquae
    caelestis patiens latus.

'What if past love came back and tied
Us teamed to the brass yoke of Venus,
If blonde Chloe were thrust outside
And jilted Lydia found the door left open wide?'

'Though he's star-bright and you're as mad
As the outrageous Adriatic
And light as cork, I'd still be glad
To live with you and die with you, come good or bad.'

10

If you were a Scythian squaw and the river
Don was your drink, you'd relent before
Letting me lie stretched out to shiver
In the blizzard beside your hard hut-door.

Can you hear the gate creak in the wind and the trees in
Your elegant villa's courtyard bower
Groan, Lyce? Feel Jupiter freezing
The fallen snow with his pure, clear power?

Venus hates pride; so enough of this hauteur,
Or the wheel may spin back and the rope go too.
No Tuscan could ever have fathered a daughter
As stiff and Penelope-cold as you.

Though you're proof against presents and prayers and the
    ashen
Cheeks of adorers ill with distress,
Unmoved by even your husband's passion
For a slut from Thessaly, nonetheless

Spare us poor suitors, O hard heart tougher
Than oak, as mild as a Moorish snake.
Not for ever will these bones suffer
The rain and the doorstep for your sake.

XI

Mercuri – nam te docilis magistro
movit Amphion lapides canendo –
tuque testudo resonare septem
    callida nervis,

nec loquax olim neque grata, nunc et
divitum mensis et amica templis,
dic modos, Lyde quibus obstinatas
    applicet auris,

quae velut latis equa trima campis
ludit exsultim metuitque tangi,
nuptiarum expers et adhuc protervo
    cruda marito.

tu potes tigris comitesque silvas
ducere et rivos celeris morari;
cessit immanis tibi blandienti
    ianitor aulae,

Cerberus, quamvis furiale centum
muniant angues caput eius atque
spiritus taeter saniesque manet
    ore trilingui.

quin et Ixion Tityosque vultu
risit invito, stetit urna paulum
sicca, dum grato Danai puellas
    carmine mulces.

audiat Lyde scelus atque notas
virginum poenas et inane lymphae
dolium fundo pereuntis imo,
    seraque fata,

11

O Mercury, who showed willing Amphion
How to transport stones by the power of music,
And you, shell of the lyre, quick to respond to
　　Touch with your seven strings,

Dumb once and unadmired, but now beloved
Guest at the banquet couch and in the temple,
Teach me a melody to make young Lyde
　　Open her stubborn ears;

She, like a three-year-old filly cavorting
Skittishly in the big fields, skips and shies from
Hands, still a stranger to the love-rite, still not
　　Ripe for an eager man.

Lyre, you can charm the tigers from the jungle,
Coax the trees with them, halt the flow of rivers;
And once you blandished Cerberus, the dreadful
　　Guard at the gates of death,

To yield his ground for all the hundred serpents
That fortify his fury-head, for all the
Foul fumes of his breath, the bloody slaver
　　Dripped from his three-tongued jaw.

Yes, even Tityos and Ixion paused and
Smiled through their anguish; for a little moment
The jugs stood dry, you sang, and the enchanted
　　Danaids knew some peace.

Let Lyde hear now of those girls' notorious
Crime and the penance – the great jar that never
Fills up with water leaking from the bottom –
　　Learn how at long last Fate

quae manent culpas etiam sub Orco.
impiae – nam quid potuere maius ? –
impiae sponsos potuere duro
　　perdere ferro.

una de multis face nuptiali
digna periurum fuit in parentem
splendide mendax et in omne virgo
　　nobilis aevum,

'surge,' quae dixit iuveni marito,
'surge, ne longus tibi somnus, unde
non times, detur; socerum et scelestas
　　falle sorores,

quae velut nactae vitulos leaenae
singulos eheu lacerant: ego illis
mollior nec te feriam neque intra
　　claustra tenebo.

me pater saevis oneret catenis,
quod viro clemens misero peperci:
me vel extremos Numidarum in agros
　　classe releget.

i pedes quo te rapiunt et aurae,
dum favet nox et Venus, i secundo
omine et nostri memorem sepulcro
　　scalpe querelam.'

XII

Miserarum est neque amori dare ludum neque dulci
mala vino lavere, aut exanimari metuentis
　　patruae verbera linguae.

Even in Hades finds the evil-doer
Unnatural women (for what darker outrage
Could they have done?), they had the heart to slaughter
    Husbands: cold hearts, cold steel.

One bride alone, among the many, honoured
The torch of marriage, proved a shining liar
To her oath-breaking father and for all time
    Stands as a paragon.

'Arise,' she whispered to her tender bridegroom,
'Arise, lest sleep from where you least expect it,
The long, long sleep, descends. Fly from my father,
    Fly from my sisters – ah,

Vicious like she-lions that have clawed down bullocks
And maul the corpse, each savages a man now!
I am less hard than they: I cannot strike nor
    Trap you with bolts and bars.

Me let my father load with painful fetters
For taking pity on my helpless husband,
Or hurry with his navy into far-off
    Libya and banishment.

But you – go where the roads and the sea-breezes
Carry you. Night and Venus are propitious.
Go, and God speed. Remember me and carve some
    Elegy on my tomb.'

12

It's a miserable life for the girls who cannot play
The game of love, or wash their cares away
With comforting wine, a miserable life for nieces
Flayed by an uncle's tongue till their nerves are in pieces.

tibi qualum Cythereae puer ales, tibi telas
operosaeque Minervae studium aufert, Neobule,
　　Liparaei nitor Hebri,

simul unctos Tiberinis umeros lavit in undis,
eques ipso melior Bellerophonte, neque pugno
　　neque segni pede victus:

catus idem per apertum fugientis agitato
grege cervos iaculari et celer arto latitantem
　　fruticeto excipere aprum.

XIII

O fons Bandusiae splendidior vitro
dulci digne mero non sine floribus,
　　cras donaberis haedo,
　　　　cui frons turgida cornibus

primis et venerem et proelia destinat;
frustra: nam gelidos inficiet tibi
　　rubro sanguine rivos
　　　　lascivi suboles gregis.

te flagrantis atrox hora Caniculae
nescit tangere, tu frigus amabile
　　fessis vomere tauris
　　　　praebes et pecori vago.

fies nobilium tu quoque fontium,
me dicente cavis impositam ilicem
　　saxis, unde loquaces
　　　　lymphae desiliunt tuae.

Poor Neobule! Venus's boy comes flitting
In at your window and carries off your knitting,
Your wool-basket and all your resolves to be
Good at Minerva's tasks, the moment you see

Hebrus from Lipara by the banks of the Tiber strip
Oil-glistening shoulders and take his morning dip.
In the ring, on the track, fists or on foot, he's faster
Than any; mounted, he'd be Bellerophon's master;

In the hunt he's the one, when the dogs have roused the deer
In a startled herd, who kills with an accurate spear
As they dash through the open; quick, too, to face
The boar lurking in its brambled hiding-place.

13

Spring of Bandusia, whose crystalline
Glitter deserves our garlands and best wine,
    You shall be given a kid
    Tomorrow. Horns half-hid

In a bulging forehead forecast love and war –
Fine destiny, but not the one in store:
    The hot goat people's son
    Must with his crimson one

Dye your cool vein. No Dog-day in intense
August can touch the sweet chill you dispense
    To unfenced, wandering flocks
    And the plough-weary ox.

My verse shall make you too a famous spring,
Known for the ilex on the echoing
    Cavern beneath whose shade
    Your garrulous streams cascade.

XIV

Herculis ritu modo dictus, o plebs,
morte venalem petiisse laurum
Caesar Hispana repetit penatis
   victor ab ora.

unico gaudens mulier marito
prodeat iustis operata divis,
et soror clari ducis et decorae
   supplice vitta

virginum matres iuvenumque nuper
sospitum. vos, o pueri et puellae
non virum expertae, male ominatis
   parcite verbis.

hic dies vere mihi festus atras
eximet curas; ego nec tumultum
nec mori per vim metuam tenente
   Caesare terras.

i pete unguentum, puer, et coronas
et cadum Marsi memorem duelli,
Spartacum si qua potuit vagantem
   fallere testa.

dic et argutae properet Neaerae
murreum nodo cohibere crinem;
si per invisum mora ianitorem
   fiet, abito.

14

Good people, he who all men say
Resembles divine Hercules
In risking death to win the bay,
  Comes conquering from Spain
  Home to his hearth again.

When the just gods have been well paid,
Happy for her great emperor
Let Livia, his wife, parade
  Proudly, and at her side
  Our leader's sister ride,

And mothers giving thanks for young
Daughters and sons kept safe, their brows
Gay with wool ribbons. Guard your tongue,
  Boys, and, you maidens still
  Unmarried, speak no ill.

I celebrate, and with good cause,
A day that banishes dark cares.
While the world's bound by Caesar's laws.
  I need not apprehend
  War or a violent end.

Boy, fetch me wreaths, bring perfume, pour
Wine from a jar that can recall
Memories of the Marsian war
  (If any dodged the hands
  Of Spartacus' raiding bands),

And ask Neaera – she's the girl
With the sweet voice – to knot her brown
Hair and come quickly. If her churl
  Porter creates delay,
  Don't wait, leave right away.

lenit albescens animos capillus
litium et rixae cupidos protervae;
non ego hoc ferrem calidus iuventa
    consule Planco.

XV

    Uxor pauperis Ibyci,
tandem nequitiae fige modum tuae
    famosisque laboribus:
maturo propior desine funeri
    inter luderc virgincs
et stellis nebulam spargere candidis.
    non, si quid Pholoen satis,
et te, Chlori, decet: filia rectius
    expugnat iuvenum domos,
pulso Thyias uti concita tympano.
    illam cogit amor Nothi
lascivae similem ludere capreae:
    te lanae prope nobilem
tonsae Luceriam, non citharae decent
    nec flos purpureus rosae
nec poti vetulam faece tenus cadi.

XVI

Inclusam Danaen turris aenea
robustaeque fores et vigilum canum
tristes excubiae munierant satis
    nocturnis ab adulteris,

Grey hairs have cooled a heart once hot
For provocation and wild brawls.
When blood was young and boiled ... I'd not
    Have let an insult slip
    In Plancus' consulship!

15

Ibycus the poor man's wife,
Come, put an end to this disreputable life,
    These scandalous paradings.
The time is past for pirouetting with the maidens;
    You're ripening for death;
Stop clouding their bright galaxy with your grey breath.
    What Pholoe does becomes
Pholoe but not you. Like a maenad maddened by drums
    Your daughter breaks down men's doors
(Behaviour, Chloris, less appropriate when yours);
    Passion is making her gad
Like a roe on heat, her darling Nothus is driving her mad.
    You, though, should now be knitting
Lamb's wool from Luceria. That lyre is hardly fitting,
    Pink roses do not please,
Nor do those wine-jars swigged down an old throat to the lees.

16

A tower of bronze, thick oak doors, savage dogs
Awake all night and day ready to bark,
Would have sufficed to keep Danae locked up
    From lovers that prowl in the dark,

si non Acrisium virginis abditae
custodem pavidum Iuppiter et Venus
risissent: fore enim tutum iter et patens
    converso in pretium deo.

aurum per medios ire satellites
et perrumpere amat saxa potentius
ictu fulmineo: concidit auguris
    Argivi domus ob lucrum

demersa exitio: diffidit urbium
portas vir Macedo et subruit aemulos
reges muneribus; munera navium
    saevos illaqueant duces.

crescentem sequitur cura pecuniam
maiorumque fames. iure perhorrui
late conspicuum tollere verticem,
    Maecenas, equitum decus.

quanto quisque sibi plura negaverit,
ab dis plura feret: nil cupientium
nudus castra peto et transfuga divitum
    partis linquere gestio,

contemptae dominus splendidior rei
quam si quidquid arat impiger Apulus
occultare meis dicerer horreis,
    magnas inter opes inops.

purae rivus aquae silvaque iugerum
paucorum et segetis certa fides meae
fulgentem imperio fertilis Africae
    fallit sorte beatior.

quamquam nec Calabrae mella ferunt apes
nec Laestrygonia Bacchus in amphora ·
languescit mihi nec pinguia Gallicis
    crescunt vellera pascuis,

If Venus and Jupiter had not played the girl's
Fear-ridden guard, Acrisius, that funny
Trick: they knew that the way would be smoothed, made safe
   For a god in the form of money!

Gold glides past sentinels and ministers
Straight to the throne, strikes deeper into rock
Than lightning. When the Argive augur died,
   Gold engineered the shock

That ruined his house; the man from Macedon
Burst city gates, brought rival kings to grief
With a few bribes; even tough naval captains
   Run on the golden reef.

As wealth grows, worry grows, and thirst for more wealth.
Splendid Maecenas (splendid yet still a knight),
Have I not done right in ducking low to keep
   My headpiece out of sight?

The more a man denies himself, the more
God grants him. See, I go with empty hands,
Glad to desert from the ranks of the rich, to camp
   With the unself-seeking bands,

Lord of the little that other men despise,
But prouder than if I were rumoured to have in store
All the corn of labouring Apulia –
   A rich man, but a poor

Fool. My few woodland acres, my clear brook,
My crops that keep faith might – though he does not know it –
Make fertile Africa's glittering proconsul
   Envious of a poet.

Calabrian bees bring me no honey-bags,
My wine lies mellowing in no Formian jar,
I own no pastures in Cisalpine Gaul
   Where the thick fleeces are,

importuna tamen pauperies abest
nec, si plura velim, tu dare deneges.
contracto melius parva cupidine
    vectigalia porrigam,

quam si Mygdoniis regnum Alyattei
campis continuem. multa petentibus
desunt multa: bene est, cui deus obtulit
    parca quod satis est manu.

XVII

Aeli vetusto nobilis ab Lamo, –
quando et priores hinc Lamias ferunt
    denominatos et nepotum
        per memores genus omne fastus,

auctore ab illo ducis originem,
qui Formiarum moenia dicitur
    princeps et innantem Maricae
        litoribus tenuisse Lirim

late tyrannus: – cras foliis nemus
multis et alga litus inutili
    demissa tempestas ab Euro
        sternet, aquae nisi fallit augur

annosa cornix. dum potes, aridum
compone lignum: cras Genium mero
    curabis et porco bimestri
        cum famulis operum solutis.

Yet nagging poverty still keeps its distance,
And, if I needed more, you'd not refuse.
By narrowing my desires I shall enlarge
   My real revenues

Better than if I made a double kingdom
Of Phrygia and King Alyattes' land.
Who seeks shall lack. Happy to whom God gives
   Enough with a sparing hand.

17

Good friend, whose blue blood comes from the legendary
Lamus (for all those earlier Lamiae
   Took name from him, men say, and tables
     Genealogically trace the title

Down through the line) – he, then, is your ancestor
Whom people call first founder of Formiae,
   Who ruled the marshlands Liris swims through,
     Brimming the haunts of the nymph Marica:

Huge realm. Tomorrow, launched from the east, a gale
Will leave the copse thick-littered with foliage,
   The shore with seaweed waste, unless that
     Prophet of downpour, the ancient raven,

Has told a lie. So get in your burnable
Wood while you can. Come dawn, you shall pamper your
   Dear soul with young roast pig and wine, and
     Master and slaves will enjoy the day off.

XVIII

Faune, Nympharum fugientum amator,
per meos finis et aprica rura
lenis incedas abeasque parvis
   aequus alumnis,

si tener pleno cadit haedus anno,
larga nec desunt Veneris sodali
vina craterae, vetus ara multo
   fumat odore.

ludit herboso pecus omne campo,
cum tibi Nonae redeunt Decembres;
festus in pratis vacat otioso
   cum bove pagus;

inter audaces lupus errat agnos;
spargit agrestis tibi silva frondis;
gaudet invisam pepulisse fossor
   ter pede terram.

XIX

Quantum distet ab Inacho
Codrus pro patria non timidus mori,
   narras et genus Aeaci
et pugnata sacro bella sub Ilio:
   quo Chium pretio cadum
mercemur, quis aquam temperet ignibus

18

Faunus, who loves the Nymphs and makes
Them scamper, leap my boundary stakes,
Lightly and benignly pass
Across the sunny fields of grass,
Leave behind your blessing on
My lambs and kids, and so be gone.
In return receive your due:
A goat shall die to honour you
At the year's end, the ancient shrine
Smoke with thick incense, and the wine,
Liberally poured, keep filling up
Venus' friend, the drinking-cup.
When the December Nones come round,
All the farm beasts on the green ground
Gambol, and with time to spare
The world enjoys the open air,
Countryman and unyoked ox
Together; in among the flocks
Unfeared the wolf strolls; from the copse
The leaf, to be your carpet, drops;
And in three-time the son of toil
Jigs on his enemy the soil.

19

From Inachus, king of Argos the year dot,
Down to the death of that brave patriot
Codrus, you give us facts, you burden us
With the genealogy of Aeacus
And the wars that under sacred Troy were fought,
But as for details like how much we ought

quo praebente domum et quota
Paelignis caream frigoribus, taces.
   da lunae propere novae,
da noctis mediae, da, puer, auguris
   Murenae: tribus aut novem
miscentur cyathis pocula commodis.
   quis Musas amat imparis,
ternos ter cyathos attonitus petet
   vates; tris prohibet supra
rixarum metuens tangere Gratia
   nudis iuncta sororibus.
insanire iuvat: cur Berecyntiae
   cessant flamina tibiae ?
cur pendet tacita fistula cum lyra ?
   parcentis ego dexteras
odi: sparge rosas: audiat invidus
   dementem strepitum Lycus
et vicina seni non habilis Lyco.
   spissa te nitidum coma,
puro te similem, Telephe, Vespero,
   tempestiva petit Rhode:
me lentus Glycerae torret amor meae.

XX

Non vides quanto moveas periclo,
Pyrrhe, Gaetulae catulos leaenae ?
dura post paulo fugies inaudax
   proelia raptor,

cum per obstantis iuvenum catervas
ibit insignem repetens Nearchum,
grande certamen, tibi praeda cedat
   maior an illi.

To pay for Chian wine, who provides heat
For the bathwater, at whose house we meet,
And at what hour I can lock out the cold
Paelignian mountain air, no one's been told
Anything.

    Come, boy, look sharp. Let the healths rip!
To midnight! The new moon! The augurship
Of our Murena! Mix the bowls – diluted
With three or nine parts wine: tastes must be suited.
The poet, who loves the Muses' number, nine,
Inspired, demands that measure of pure wine.
The Grace, though, who goes naked, hand in hand
With her two sisters, fears brawls and has banned
More than three ladles for the plain man. Riot
Runs in my veins. Why has a sudden quiet
Fallen? Keep blowing on the Phrygian flute!
Why let the pipe hang there beside the mute
Lyre on the wall? I hate a miser's fist.
Fling roses! Let the old misanthropist
Lycus next door and that girl he enjoys
(Incongruous couple) wake at our wild noise.
Telephus, as radiant with your glossy curls
As the evening star, Rhode is yours – the girl's
Ripe and pursues you. As for me, desire
For Glycera still burns, long, fierce, slow fire.

20

    Pyrrhus, surely you realise
    How foolhardy it is to prise
    Cubs from an African lioness?
Soon you'll be dodging sharp claws, less
A raider than a runaway, when
Clean through the thicket of young men
She sails to find her handsome pet
Nearchus, and the stage is set
For an epic struggle: will you take,

interim, dum tu celeris sagittas
promis, haec dentis acuit timendos,
   arbiter pugnae posuisse nudo
     sub pede palmam

fertur et leni recreare vento
sparsum odoratis umerum capillis,
   qualis aut Nireus fuit aut aquosa
     raptus ab Ida.

XXI

O nata mecum consule Manlio,
seu tu querelas sive geris iocos
   seu rixam et insanos amores
     seu facilem, pia testa, somnum,

quocumque lectum nomine Massicum
servas, moveri digna bono die,
   descende, Corvino iubente
     promere languidiora vina.

non ille, quamquam Socraticis madet
sermonibus, te negleget horridus:
   narratur et prisci Catonis
     saepe mero caluisse virtus.

tu lene tormentum ingenio admoves
plerumque duro; tu sapientium
   curas et arcanum iocoso
     consilium retegis Lyaeo;

Or can she keep, the prize at stake?
But while she whets ferocious teeth
And you stand groping in your sheath
For arrows to send whizzing out,
The arbiter of this great bout,
Look, has walked off, trampling the palm
Beneath bare feet, and lets the calm
Breeze cool his shoulders fringed with strands
Of perfumed hair. So there he stands
Like Nireus or the boy the books
Tell us Jove kidnapped for his looks
From Ida of the thousand brooks.

21

Wine-jar whose birth-year, Manlius' consulship,
Was mine as well, unstopper of elegies,
    Jokes, quarrels, love's crazed fits and blessed
        Effortless slumber (your kindest office),

You've kept the choice old Massic in store for a
Great moment: now, whatever occasion you
    Foresaw, descend like Jove – my guest has
        Called for a mellower wine from upstairs.

His drink is Plato's wisdom of Socrates –
Deep tipple; yet he'll never uncivilly
    Snub *you*: they say old Cato often
        Warmed his morale with an undiluted

Cup. Jar, you put brains stolid by nature to
Torment on your sweet rack; the philosopher's
    Dark thoughts are bared, most secret counsels
        Spilled at the prompting of jolly Bacchus;

tu spem reducis mentibus anxiis,
virisque et addis cornua pauperi
    post te neque iratos trementi
        regum apices neque militum arma.

te Liber et, si laeta aderit, Venus
segnesque nodum solvere Gratiae
    vivaeque producent lucernae,
        dum rediens fugat astra Phoebus.

XXII

Montium custos nemorumque, Virgo,
quae laborantis utero puellas
    ter vocata audis adimisque leto,
        diva triformis,

imminens villae tua pinus esto,
quam per exactos ego laetus annos
verris obliquum meditantis ictum
    sanguine donem.

XXIII

Caelo supinas si tuleris manus
nascente Luna, rustica Phidyle,
    si ture placaris et horna
        fruge Lares avidaque porca,

nec pestilentem sentiet Africum
fecunda vitis nec sterilem seges
    robiginem aut dulces alumni
        pomifero grave tempus anno.

You rally lost hopes back to the worry-worn,
You bring the poor man courage and confidence:
   Crowned kings can rage, call out their soldiers –
    After a taste of you, he'll defy them.

Friends keep you up late: Liber with Venus, when
She's gay, the three linked Graces who hate to let
   Go hands, and bright lamps burning on till
    Phoebus, returning, defeats the starlight.

22

Friend of hills and woody places,
Goddess of three shapes and faces,
   Virgin, when summonéd
   Thrice by young wives in childbed,
Givest ear to the hard-pressed
And from death deliverest,
   Henceforth I declare this pine
   Shadowing my villa, thine.
Blood of a wild boar that's just
Aiming his first sidelong thrust
   Shall at each year's turning be
   Gladly given to it by me.

23

Hold out your hands, palms turned to the sky, when the
New moon is up, my country-bred Phidyle;
   Treat well the Lars: bring incense, this year's
    Corn and your greediest pig to please them.

Do this and you'll have vines that the pestilent
Siroccos bypass, crops that the rust cannot
   Rot, bonny newborn beasts that autumn,
    Season of murrain and apples, lets live.

nam quae nivali pascitur Algido
devota quercus inter et ilices
   aut crescit Albanis in herbis
     victima pontificum securis

cervice tinget: te nihil attinet
temptare multa caede bidentium
   parvos coronantem marino
     rore deos fragilique myrto.

immunis aram si tetigit manus
non sumptuosa blandior hostia,
   mollivit aversos Penatis
     farre pio et saliente mica.

XXIV

Intactis opulentior
thesauris Arabum et divitis Indiae
   caementis licet occupes
Tyrrhenum omne tuis et mare publicum,
   si figit adamantinos
summis verticibus dira Necessitas
   clavos, non animum metu,
non mortis laqueis expedies caput.
   campestres melius Scythae,
quorum plaustra vagas rite trahunt domos,
   vivunt et rigidi Getae,
immetata quibus iugera liberas
   fruges et Cererem ferunt,
nec cultura placet longior annua,
   defunctumque laboribus
aequali recreat sorte vicarius.
   illic matre carentibus
privignis mulier temperat innocens,

Somewhere on snow-topped Algidus, deep among
Ilex and oak, or stretching its neck to graze
   Lake Alba's girth-increasing grasses,
      Wanders the animal doomed to dye red

The pontiff's axe. No need for my Phidyle
To organise incarnadined hecatombs:
   She weaves for her small gods the garlands
      Rosemary graces or fragile myrtle.

Pure, empty hands touch altars as closely as
Those heaping dear-bought offerings. Simple gifts
   Soothe angry household gods: the poor man's
      Sputtering salt and his cake of plain meal.

24

You who are richer than
The unplundered treasure-chests of the Arabian
   Sheikhs and the rajah kings,
Who build up all the land and thrust your scaffoldings
   Into the public sea,
Beware! Once on your gable grim Necessity
   Her adamant nails has set,
Soul shall feel terror, flesh shall not escape death's net.
   The Scythians of the plains,
People whose wandering houses travel upon wains,
   Live better, and the tough
Getae whose unmarked acres furnish food enough
   For common need: their men
Each labour on the land for a year only, then
   By equal rote another's
Willing to take his turn; no merciless stepmothers
   Harry poor orphans there,

    nec dotata regit virum
coniunx nec nitido fidit adultero.
    dos est magna parentium
virtus et metuens alterius viri
    certo foedere castitas;
et peccare nefas aut pretium est mori.
    o quisquis volet impias
caedis et rabiem tollere civicam,
    si quaeret 'pater urbium'
subscribi statuis, indomitam audeat
    refrenare licentiam,
clarus postgenitis: quatenus – heu nefas! –
    virtutem incolumem odimus,
sublatam ex oculis quaerimus invidi.
    quid tristes querimoniae,
si non supplicio culpa reciditur,
    quid leges sine moribus
vanae proficiunt, si neque fervidis
    pars inclusa caloribus
mundi nec Boreae finitimum latus
    durataeque solo nives
mercatorem abigunt, horrida callidi
    vincunt aequora navitae ?
magnum pauperies opproprium iubet
    quidvis et facere et pati
virtutisque viam deserit arduae.
    vel nos in Capitolium,
quo clamor vocat et turba faventium,
    vel nos in mare proximum
gemmas et lapides, aurum et inutile,
    summi materiem mali,
mittamus, scelerum si bene paenitet.
    eradenda cupidinis
pravi sunt elementa et tenerae nimis
    mentes asperioribus
formandae studiis. nescit equo rudis
    haerere ingenuus puer
venarique timet, ludere doctior

No wives govern by dowry or lean on debonair
   Young lovers. Family pride
Is their rich dower, chastity shy to glance aside,
   Faith in the marriage tie;
Sin is abhorred; the price of scandal is to die.
   He who would cleanse the State
Of bloodshed and the civil fury the gods hate
   And be on statues styled
'Father of Cities', let him be brave, bridle our wild
   Licence and stake his fame
With the next generation: we, to our deep shame,
   Envy and hate the sight
Of virtue (though we're quick to mourn its vanished light).
   Why raise these tragic sighs
When evil, still unpruned by punishment, multiplies?
   What are our vain laws worth
Without morality, now that no place on earth
   – Not even the tropic belt
Or the borders of the Pole where the snows never melt –
   Bars traders, and no sea
Heaves that can foil our seamen's ingenuity?
   Since to be poor's a great
Dishonour now, poverty bids men tolerate
   Anything, dare all crimes,
And turns aside from the steep path that Virtue climbs.
   To the Capitol let us bring
Our jewels, our gauds, our gold (that useless, deadly thing,
   The matter and the cause
Of our great ill) and thereby win all Rome's applause,
   Or, if we'd truly be
Repentant, toss our treasures in the nearest sea.
   We must pull up by the root
The first sick growth of greed, and that too delicate shoot,
   The mind, must be made stern
By harsher disciplines. No freeborn boy will learn
   To sit a horse these days.
Hunting scares him; master of frivolous arts, he plays
   Greek hoops, or, if you'd rather,

seu Graeco iubeas trocho
seu malis vetita legibus alea,
   cum periura patris fides
consortem socium fallat et hospites,
   indignoque pecuniam
heredi properet. scilicet improbae
   crescunt divitiae; tamen
curtae nescio quid semper abest rei.

XXV

Quo me, Bacche, rapis tui
plenum ? quae nemora aut quos agor in specus
   velox mente nova ? quibus
antris egregii Caesaris audiar
   aeternum meditans decus
stellis inserere et consilio Iovis ?
   dicam insigne recens adhuc
indictum ore alio. non secus in iugis
   exsomnis stupet Euhias
Hebrum prospiciens et nive candidam
   Thracen ac pede barbaro
lustratam Rhodopen, ut mihi devio
   ripas et vacuum nemus
mirari libet. o Naiadum potens
   Baccharumque valentium
proceras manibus vertere fraxinos,
   nil parvum aut humili modo,
nil mortale loquar. dulce periculum est,
   o Lenaee, sequi deum
cingentem viridi tempora pampino.

Rolls dice against the law: no wonder, for his father
    Breaks promises, mis-spends
His business partner's capital, hoodwinks his friends
    And busily puts by
Money for an unworthy heir. One can't deny
    He makes his vile wealth breed;
Yet, lacking something else, he feels a nameless need.

25

Bacchus, where am I ? Flushed
With god, to what groves, caves, am I being rushed
    Inspired ? What rocks shall hear
Me shape a poem to set great Caesar's peer-
    less glory with the high
Council of Jove, a new star in the sky ?
    Some freshly hatched, supreme
Achievement, still unmouthed, shall be my theme.
    As the wild reveller,
Sleepless and marvelling, pauses on a spur
    To gaze at Thrace, all snow,
The Hebrus and Mount Rhodope's plateau
    Tracked by barbarian feet,
I wander in a rapture off the beat-
    en path, by brooks, through trees
Where no one goes. God of the Naiades,
    God of the bacchanal bands
Who can uproot tall ash-trees with bare hands,
    I plan no homespun, slight
Or earthbound song. Welcome, the sweet delight
    Of danger! Lord of Wine,
Lead on! I follow, crowned with your green vine.

XXVI

Vixi puellis nuper idoneus
et militavi non sine gloria;
    nunc arma defunctumque bello
      barbiton hic paries habebit,

laevum marinae qui Veneris latus
custodit. hic, hic ponite lucida
    funalia et vectis et arcus
      oppositis foribus minaces.

o quae beatam diva tenes Cyprum et
Memphin carentem Sithonia nive,
    regina, sublimi flagello
      tange Chloen semel arrogantem.

XXVII

Impios parrae recinentis omen
ducat et praegnas canis aut ab agro
rava decurrens lupa Lanuvino
    fetaque vulpes:

rumpat et serpens iter institutum
si per obliquum similis sagittae
terruit mannos: ego cui timebo
    providus auspex,

26

In love's wars I have long maintained
Good fighting trim and even gained
   Some glory. But now lyre
   And veteran sword retire

And the left wall in the temple of
The sea-born deity of love
   Shall house them. Come lay, here,
   Lay down the soldier's gear –

The crowbar, the tar-blazing torch,
The bow for forcing past the porch.
   Here is my last request:
   Goddess, ruler of blest

Cyprus and Memphis, shrine that knows
No shiver of Sithonian snows,
   Whose whip bends proud girls' knees –
   One flick for Chloe, please.

27

May evil men be sped with evil omens –
A screeching owl, a pregnant bitch, a vixen
Swollen with cubs, or a grey she-wolf lolloping
   Down from Lanuvium –

And may their journey stop as soon as started,
When a snake arrowing sideways sends the ponies
Panicking. But for those I feel concern for
   I shall perform the good

antequam stantis repetat paludes
imbrium divina avis imminentum,
oscinem corvum prece suscitabo
    solis ab ortu.

sis licet felix ubicumque mavis,
et memor nostri, Galatea, vivas,
teque nec laevus vetet ire picus
    nec vaga cornix.

sed vides quanto trepidet tumultu
pronus Orion. ego quid sit ater
Hadriae novi sinus et quid albus
    peccet Iapyx.

hostium uxores puerique caecos
sentiant motus orientis Austri et
aequoris nigri fremitum et trementis
    verbere ripas.

sic et Europe niveum doloso
credidit tauro latus et scatentem
beluis pontum mediasque fraudes
    palluit audax.

nuper in pratis studiosa florum et
debitae Nymphis opifex coronae,
nocte sublustri nihil astra praeter
    vidit et undas.

quae simul centum tetigit potentem
oppidis Cretan, 'pater, o relictum
filiae nomen, pietasque' dixit
    'victa furore!

unde quo veni ? levis una mors est
virginum culpae. vigilansne ploro
turpe commissum, an vitiis carentem
    ludit imago

Office of augur and entreat the wise-voiced
Raven to caw good weather from the sunrise
Before he flies home to his marshy pools to
    Prophesy pouring rain.

Then go, my Galatea, and, wherever
You choose, live happily; do not forget me.
No stray crow or woodpecker darting leftwards
    Keep you indoors today!

But, look, Orion sinks low in a welter
Of storm. I know of old the Adriatic's
Black mischief, and how wicked the north-wester's
    Innocent skies can be.

The blind crescendo of a southerly hurricane,
Loud, pitch-black breakers and stunned, buffeted beaches
Are an ordeal that I would only wish on
    Enemies' wives and sons.

Another girl, remember, who entrusted
Her white legs to the sly bull, discovered
Danger and monsters in mid-sea: Europa,
    Pale in her recklessness,

Who in the fields that morning, all her mind on
Flowers, had composed the Nymphs a votive garland,
That night discerned in glimmering half-darkness
    Nothing but waves and stars.

To Crete she came, isle of the hundred cities,
And there she cried, 'Father, I have abandoned
The name and duties of a daughter. Madness
    Mastered me. Farewell, home,

For a strange land – sorry exchange! One death is
Too light a punishment for a guilty virgin.
Am I awake? Is the bad deed I weep for
    Done, or was I misled

vana, quae porta fugiens eburna
somnium ducit? meliusne fluctus
ire per longos fuit, an recentis
   carpere flores?

si quis infamem mihi nunc iuvencum
dedat iratae, lacerare ferro et
frangere enitar modo multum amati
   cornua monstri.

impudens liqui patrios Penatis,
impudens Orcum moror. o deorum
si quis haec audis, utinam inter errem
   nuda leones!

antequam turpis macies decentis
occupet malas teneraeque sucus
defluat praedae, speciosa quaero
   pascere tigris.

"vilis Europe," pater urget absens:
"quid mori cessas? potes hac ab orno
pendulum zona bene te secuta
   laedere collum.

sive te rupes et acuta leto
saxa delectant, age te procellae
crede veloci, nisi erile mavis
   carpere pensum

regius sanguis, dominaeque tradi
barbarae paelex."' aderat querenti
perfidum ridens Venus et remisso
   filius arcu.

mox, ubi lusit satis: 'abstineto'
dixit 'irarum calidaeque rixae,
cum tibi invisus laceranda reddet
   cornua taurus.

In innocence by a false dream-peddling phantom
Slipped through the Ivory Gate? Should I have voyaged
The long sea-miles or stayed and picked spring flowers?
   Easy to choose too late!

Deliver up that young bull to my vengeance,
And with a sword I'll hew him piecemeal, hack off
The horns of that abominable monster
   Loved with such passion once.

Dead to all shame, I left my household gods; now
Shameless again, I keep Death waiting. O hear me,
Some god in heaven, and sentence me to walk stripped
   Naked among wild beasts.

Before disease and age have made a breach in
These comely cheeks, before the juice of youth dries,
While the victim is still tender, let my beauty
   Bleed on the tiger's tooth.

Far off I hear my father scolding: "Worthless
Child, why so long about your dying? That ash-tree
Will serve for hanging. Use your sash, a handy
   Friend of the maid in need;

Or, if you crave a sharper execution,
Go to the precipice and consign your body
To the wild air and the rocks, unless you'd rather
   Work at your weight of wool

For a foreign wife – a slave princess, a cast-off
Strumpet!"' Distraught, the girl looked round her. There stood
Venus, smiling her tricky smile, and with her
   Cupid, his bow unstrung.

When she had been well entertained, the goddess
Said, 'Curb your tantrums. You may be less angry
When the detested bull lays in those would-be
   Murdering hands his horns.

uxor invicti Iovis esse nescis:
mitte singultus, bene ferre magnam
disce fortunam; tua sectus orbis
   nomina ducet.'

XXVIII

  Festo quid potius die
Neptuni faciam? prome reconditum,
  Lyde, strenua Caecubum
munitaeque adhibe vim sapientiae.
  inclinare meridiem
sentis ac, veluti stet volucris dies,
  parcis deripere horreo
cessantem Bibuli consulis amphoram.
  nos cantabimus invicem
Neptunum et viridis Nereidum comas;
  tu curva recines lyra
Latonam et celeris spicula Cynthiae,
  summo carmine, quae Cnidon
fulgentisque tenet Cyclades et Paphum
  iunctis visit oloribus;
dicetur merita Nox quoque nenia.

Know you have been the bride of Jove almighty.
Come, dry those tears and learn to bear high honour
Becomingly; a continent shall henceforth
  Carry Europa's name.'

28

  What better way,
Lyde, to celebrate the festal day
  Of Neptune than
Uncupboarding the hoarded Caecuban?
  Come, girl, don't wait;
On with the siege of wisdom's fortress gate!
  The shadows grow,
The afternoon wears on, and yet, as though
  Time could not fly
And stood stock-still, you let the wine-jar lie
  (Old Bibulus
The consul's vintage) tantalising us.
  One answering
The other, we'll take turns. First I shall sing
  The god of the seas
And the green locks of the Nereides;
  Then you shall take
The curved lyre to praise Leto and to make
  Music in honour
Of Cynthia, the sharp shooter and fleet runner;
  Last, a joint song
For her to whom the Cnidian shrines belong,
  Queen of the bright
Cycladic isles, who on her swan-drawn flight
  To Paphos goes.
Night too shall have her hymn: the fitting close.

XXIX

Tyrrhena regum progenies, tibi
non ante verso lene merum cado
　　cum flore, Maecenas, rosarum et
　　　　pressa tuis balanus capillis

iamdudum apud me est. eripe te morae,
nec semper udum Tibur et Aefulae
　　declive contempleris arvum et
　　　　Telegoni iuga parricidae.

fastidiosam desere copiam et
molem propinquam nubibus arduis;
　　omitte mirari beatae
　　　　fumum et opes strepitumque Romae.

plerumque gratae divitibus vices
mundaeque parvo sub lare pauperum
　　cenae sine aulaeis et ostro
　　　　sollicitam explicuere frontem.

iam clarus occultum Andromedae pater
ostendit ignem, iam Procyon furit
　　et stella vesani Leonis,
　　　　sole dies referente siccos:

iam pastor umbras cum grege languido
rivumque fessus quaerit et horridi
　　dumeta Silvani, caretque
　　　　ripa vagis taciturna ventis.

tu civitatem quis deceat status
curas et Urbi sollicitus times
　　quid Seres et regnata Cyro
　　　　Bactra parent Tanaisque discors.

29

Descendant of Etruscan kings, Maecenas,
A jar of mellow wine still to be tilted,
  Choice roses, Syrian oil
Prepared expressly for your hair, all wait

Patiently in my house. Bestir yourself, then!
Why gaze all year towards the brooks of Tibur,
  Aefula's sloping fields
And the high hilltop which the parricide

Telegonus built? Leave your unpleasing plenty,
Leave your cloud-grazing palace, leave admiring
  The glamour of great Rome –
The money and the hubbub and the smoke.

Change for the rich can be a kind of pleasure,
And a plain meal well served in a poor cottage
  (Bare walls, no purple cloth)
Often unties the lines that worry knits.

Now shining Cepheus hoists his constellation
Up from the dark, now Procyon and Leo,
  Fierce, heat-heralding stars,
Glare as the sun brings back the days of drought;

The weary shepherd with his spent flock makes for
Shadow and water and the shaggy wood-god's
  Thickets; the river-bank
Dumbly endures the absence of the breeze.

Yet still you labour to perfect the pattern
Of government, Rome's anxious sentry keeping
  Watch on the farthest East,
Cyrus' old kingdom and the uneasy Don

prudens futuri temporis exitum
caliginosa nocte premit deus,
    ridetque si mortalis ultra
        fas trepidat. quod adest memento

componere aequus; cetera fluminis
ritu feruntur, nunc medio alveo
    cum pace delabentis Etruscum
        in mare, nunc lapides adesos

stirpesque raptas et pecus et domos
volventis una non sine montium
    clamore vicinaeque silvae,
        cum fera diluvies quietos

irritat amnis. ille potens sui
laetusque deget, cui licet in diem
    dixisse 'vixi: cras vel atra
        nube polum Pater occupato

vel sole puro; non tamen irritum,
quodcumque retro est, efficiet neque
    diffinget infectumque reddet,
        quod fugiens semel hora vexit.'

Fortuna saevo laeta negotio et
ludum insolentem ludere pertinax
    transmutat incertos honores,
        nunc mihi, nunc alii benigna.

laudo manentem; si celeris quatit
pennas, resigno quae dedit et mea
    virtute me involvo probamque
        pauperiem sine dote quaero.

non est meum, si mugiat Africis
malus procellis, ad miseras preces
    decurrere et votis pacisci
        ne Cypriae Tyriaeque merces

For plots of war. God, though, has wisely locked up
The outcome in impenetrable darkness,
   And laughs when mortals show
Inquisitive apprehension. I commend

A level mind that grapples with what's here now.
As for the rest, look on it as a river,
   One moment calm and tame,
Gliding to meet the Tuscan sea, the next

Churning a chaos of gouged rocks, torn tree-trunks,
Corpses and rubble of houses, while the mountains
   And forests amplify
The roar and pitiless rain exacerbates

The temper of the water. Call him happy
And lord of his own soul who every evening
   Can say, 'Today I have lived.
Tomorrow Jove may blot the sky with cloud

Or fill it with pure sunshine, yet he cannot
Devalue what has once been held as precious,
   Or tarnish or melt back
The gold the visiting hour has left behind.'

Fortune enjoys her grim work and will never
Give up the cruel game she plays of changing
   Her mind and her rewards:
She loves me, then she loves me not, woos him.

I praise her when she's by, but let her stretch those
Wings, I write off her gifts as losses, pull on
   Philosophy's cloak and court
Poverty, who brings no dowry but is true.

To grovel in prayer because the mast is groaning
Under the gale is not my style; I will not
   Haggle with heaven: 'God save
My bales from Tyre and Cyprus lest they go

addant avaro divitias mari.
tunc me biremis praesidio scaphae
  tutum per Aegaeos tumultus
    aura feret geminusque Pollux.

XXX

Exegi monumentum aere perennius
regalique situ pyramidum altius,
quod non imber edax, non Aquilo impotens
possit diruere aut innumerabilis
annorum series et fuga temporum.
non omnis moriar, multaque pars mei
vitabit Libitinam: usque ego postera
crescam laude recens, dum Capitolium
scandet cum tacita virgine pontifex.
dicar, qua violens obstrepit Aufidus
et qua pauper aquae Daunus agrestium
regnavit populorum, ex humili potens
princeps Aeolium carmen ad Italos
deduxisse modos. sume superbiam
quaesitam meritis et mihi Delphica
lauro cinge volens, Melpomene, comam.

To swell the greedy sea's collection!' I just
Bob through the storms of the Aegean, safely
   Tucked in my rowing-boat,
Sped by the weather and the Heavenly Twins.

30

More durable than bronze, higher than Pharaoh's
Pyramids is the monument I have made,
A shape that angry wind or hungry rain
Cannot demolish, nor the innumerable
Ranks of the years that march in centuries.
I shall not wholly die: some part of me
Will cheat the goddess of death, for while High Priest
And Vestal climb our Capitol in a hush,
My reputation shall keep green and growing.
Where Aufidus growls torrentially, where once,
Lord of a dry kingdom, Daunus ruled
His rustic people, I shall be renowned
As one who, poor-born, rose and pioneered
A way to fit Greek rhythms to our tongue.
Be proud, Melpomene, for you deserve
What praise I have, and unreluctantly
Garland my forehead with Apollo's laurel.

Q
HORATI
FLACCI
CARMINUM
LIBER QUARTUS

THE ODES OF
HORACE
BOOK
FOUR

I

Intermissa, Venus, diu
rursus bella moves? parce precor, precor.
   non sum qualis eram bonae
sub regno Cinarae. desine, dulcium
   mater saeva Cupidinum,
circa lustra decem flectere mollibus
   iam durum imperiis: abi
quo blandae iuvenum te revocant preces.
   tempestivius in domum
Pauli purpureis ales oloribus
   comissabere Maximi,
si torrere iecur quaeris idoneum:
   namque et nobilis et decens
et pro sollicitis non tacitus reis
   et centum puer artium
late signa feret militiae tuae,
   et, quandoque potentior
largi muneribus riserit aemuli,
   Albanos prope te lacus
ponet marmoream sub trabe citrea.
   illic plurima naribus
duces tura, lyraeque et Berecyntiae
   delectabere tibiae
mixtis carminibus non sine fistula;
   illic bis pueri die
numen cum teneris virginibus tuum
   laudantes pede candido
in morem Salium ter quatient humum.
   me nec femina nec puer
iam nec spes animi credula mutui
   nec certare iuvat mero
nec vincire novis tempora floribus.
   sed cur heu, Ligurine, cur
manat rara meas lacrima per genas?

1

Must it be war again
After so long a truce ? Venus, be kind, refrain,
    I beg you. The time's over
When Cinara was my gracious queen and I her lover.
    Fifty years, pitiless
Mother of the sweet Loves, weigh hard. You must not press
    This old tough-jointed horse
To run to your cajoling order round the course.
    Leave me. Go back to where
The young men call for you with a persuasive prayer.
    To Paulus Maximus' house
Pilot your lustrous swans, in proper style carouse,
    And, seeing you desire
A hot and likely heart, choose his to set on fire.
    Handsome, blue-blooded, young,
He for his nervous clients wields a ready tongue;
    He knows a hundred arts
To spread your army's banners to remotest parts;
    And when some rival, free
With lavish presents, fails, grateful and jubilant he
    Shall by the Alban lake
Beneath a cedar roof your image in marble make.
    Thick incense you'll inhale,
Sweet to your nostrils, there, and music shall regale
    Your ears – concerted lute
And curly Berecynthian pipe and shepherd's flute.
    With the sun's earliest rays
And latest boys and girls shall give your godhead praise,
    Flashing their snow-white feet,
Dancing the Salian dance, treading the triple beat.
    These days I take no joy
In the naïve hope of mutual love with woman or boy,
    Or drinking bouts with men,
Or garlanding my temples with fresh flowers. Why then,

    cur facunda parum decoro
inter verba cadit lingua silentio ?
    nocturnis ego somniis
iam captum teneo, iam volucrem sequor
    te per gramina Martii
campi, te per aquas, dure, volubilis.

II

Pindarum quisquis studet aemulari,
Iule, ceratis ope Daedalea
nititur pennis vitreo daturus
    nomina ponto.

monte decurrens velut amnis, imbres
quem super notas aluere ripas,
fervet immensusque ruit profundo
    Pindarus ore,

laurea donandus Apollinari,
seu per audaces nova dithyrambos
verba devolvit numerisque fertur
    lege solutis,

seu deos regesque canit, deorum
sanguinem, per quos cecidere iusta
morte Centauri, cecidit tremendae
    flamma Chimaerae,

sive quos Elea domum reducit
palma caelestis pugilemve equumve
dicit et centum potiore signis
    munere donat,

My Ligurinus, why
Should the reluctant-flowing tears surprise these dry
   Cheeks, and my fluent tongue
Stumble in unbecoming silences among
   Syllables? In dreams at night
I hold you in my arms, or toil behind your flight
   Across the Martian Field,
Or chase through yielding waves the boy who will not yield.

2

Julus, whoever tries to rival Pindar,
Flutters on wings of wax, a rude contriver
Doomed like the son of Daedalus to christen
   Somewhere a shining sea.

A river bursts its banks and rushes down a
Mountain with uncontrollable momentum,
Rain-saturated, churning, chanting thunder –
   There you have Pindar's style,

Who earns Apollo's diadem of laurel
In all his moods: whether he rides a torrent
Of dithyrambs, where new words swirl and headlong
   Rhythms defy the rules;

Or hymns the gods and sons of gods – heroic
Theseus who dealt the Centaurs death and justice,
Bellerophon who quenched the great Chimaera's
   Terrible, fiery face;

Or lauds the victor, charioteer or boxer,
Who, taking the palm at Pisa, in a god-like
Ecstasy wanders home, treasuring more than
   Statues the honour won;

flebili sponsae iuvenemve raptum
plorat et viris animumque moresque
aureos educit in astra nigroque
    invidet Orco.

multa Dircaeum levat aura cycnum,
tendit, Antoni, quotiens in altos
nubium tractus: ego apis Matinae
    more modoque

grata carpentis thyma per laborem
plurimum circa nemus uvidique
Tiburis ripas operosa parvus
    carmina fingo.

concines maiore poeta plectro
Caesarem, quandoque trahet feroces
per sacrum clivum merita decorus
    fronde Sygambros,

quo nihil maius meliusve terris
fata donavere bonique divi
nec dabunt, quamvis redeant in aurum
    tempora priscum.

concines laetosque dies et Urbis
publicum ludum super impetrato
fortis Augusti reditu forumque
    litibus orbum.

tum meae, si quid loquar audiendum,
vocis accedet bona pars, et, 'o Sol
pulcher! o laudande!' canam, recepto
    Caesare felix.

tuque dum procedis, 'io Triumphe!'
non semel dicemus, 'io Triumphe!'
civitas omnis, dabimusque divis
    tura benignis.

Or frames a dirge for the dead youth whose bride is
Weeping, and rears a star-high panegyric
To his magnanimity and golden virtues,
   Grudging the dark such light.

Julus Antonius, the Swan of Dirce
Felt a great wind of inspiration blowing
On which to ride the sky and visit cloudland.
   I, who resemble more

The small laborious bee from Mount Matinus
Gathering from Tibur's rivery environs
The thyme it loves, find it as hard to build up
   Poems as honeycombs.

You, who can better compass the grand manner,
Shall sing the wearer of the well-earned garland
Dragging the fierce Sygambri down the Via
   Sacra – I mean our great

Augustus: a more gracious visitation
The Fates and the good gods have never sent men,
Nor ever shall again, though time, turned backwards,
   Run, as of old, to gold.

Sing of our holidays, the City's public
Games to acclaim the conquering hero coming
Home as our prayers desired, sing of the Forum
   Empty of lawsuits now.

Then I, if I can find words worth attention,
Will chime in with the best voice I can muster,
Hailing the day, the halcyon and hurrahing
   Sun that brings Caesar back.

And while you walk in front we'll shout together
'Io Triumphe!', the whole populace clamouring
'Io Triumphe!', offering the incense
   Due to the kindly gods.

te decem tauri totidemque vaccae,
me tener solvet vitulus, relicta
matre qui largis iuvenescit herbis
    in mea vota,

fronte curvatos imitatus ignis
tertium lunae referentis ortum,
qua notam duxit, niveus videri,
    cetera fulvus.

III

Quem tu, Melpomene, semel
nascentem placido lumine videris,
    illum non labor Isthmius
clarabit pugilem, non equus impiger
    curru ducet Achaico
victorem, neque res bellica Deliis
    ornatum foliis ducem,
quod regum tumidas contuderit minas,
    ostendet Capitolio:
sed quae Tibur aquae fertile praefluunt
    et spissae nemorum comae
fingent Aeolio carmine nobilem.
    Romae principis urbium
dignatur suboles inter amabilis
    vatum ponere me choros,
et iam dente minus mordeor invido.
    o, testudinis aureae
dulcem quae strepitum, Pieri, temperas,
    o mutis quoque piscibus
donatura cycni, si libeat, sonum,
    totum muneris hoc tui est,
quod monstror digito praetereuntium
    Romanae fidicen lyrae:
quod spiro et placeo, si placeo, tuum est.

Ten bulls, ten cows you swore for his home-coming;
A young calf will acquit my vow. New-weaned and
Cropping the thick green grass, it grows to meet its
   Destiny and my debt,

With two slim horns like those the young moon shows us
Curving in heaven on her third night of rising,
And one eye-catching, snow-white splash; its body
   Tawny except for that.

3

   He whose nativity
Your shining eye has blessed, Melpomene,
   Shall be no pugilist
Famed at the Isthmus for his flailing fist;
   No fleet-horsed racing-car,
Greek-style, shall pull him past the post, no war
   Crown him with Delian bays,
A captain flaunted to the Capitol's gaze,
   Or make his name renowned
For grinding arrogant emperors to the ground.
   But tree-tops overhead,
Thick-foliaged, and the rivulets that thread
   Tibur shall forge him strong
Prestige as master of Aeolian song.
   Now that the paramount
City on earth's children have deigned to count
   Me with the happy ring
Of lyric poets, less sharp is envy's sting.
   Maid of the sacred well,
Who tunes the sweet clash of the golden shell
   And might, should you so wish,
With the swan's music dower the dumb fish,
   Your gift it is that I
Walk pointed out by every passer-by –
   'Rome's poet'; thanks to you
That I compose and please, if please I do.

IV

Qualem ministrum fulminis alitem,
cui rex deorum regnum in avis vagas
   permisit expertus fidelem
     Iuppiter in Ganymede flavo,

olim iuventas et patrius vigor
nido laborum protulit inscium,
   vernique iam nimbis remotis
     insolitos docuere nisus

venti paventem, mox in ovilia
demisit hostem vividus impetus,
   nunc in reluctantis dracones
     egit amor dapis atque pugnae,

qualemve laetis caprea pascuis
intenta fulvae matris ab ubere
   iam lacte depulsum leonem
     dente novo peritura vidit,

videre Raeti bella sub Alpibus
Drusum gerentem Vindelici – quibus
   mos unde deductus per omne
     tempus Amazonia securi

dextras obarmet, quaerere distuli,
nec scire fas est omnia – sed diu
   lateque victrices catervae
     consiliis iuvenis revictae

sensere, quid mens rite, quid indoles
nutrita faustis sub penetralibus
   posset, quid Augusti paternus
     in pueros animus Nerones.

4

Have you seen the feathered servant of the lightning,
Made by the king of gods king of his wandering
    Kind for his trusty part
In kidnapping the blond boy Ganymede?

Young blood and eagle's energy first launch him
Out of the nest to meet a sky of troubles,
    And the spring winds conspire,
Now storms are past, to teach his timid wings

Airy adventures. Soon his great sweep sends him
Plummeting down to terrify the sheepfold,
    Or, rage- and hunger-driven,
He lugs the wrestling serpent in his grip.

Have you seen a roe-deer browsing in contentment,
And then a lion whelp come upon her, freshly
    Weaned from the tawny teat –
Doomed she looks up, food for his unfleshed tooth?

Eagle or lion was Drusus to the warring
Vindelici among the Rhaetian passes,
    Whose right hands have preferred
The Amazon axe from immemorial time

(Custom whose origin we cannot guess here,
Nor should men sound all knowledge). Long unconquered,
    Victors on many fields,
Their armes scattered by a young man's skill

Have learnt what power accrues when mind and heart are
Fed with religion in a reverent household,
    Learnt what paternal love
Can do, when it is Caesar's, for two boys.

fortes creantur fortibus et bonis;
est in iuvencis, est in equis patrum
   virtus, neque imbellem feroces
     progenerant aquilae columbam;

doctrina sed vim promovet insitam,
rectique cultus pectora roborant:
   utcumque defecere mores,
     indecorant bene nata culpae.

quid debeas, o Roma, Neronibus,
testis Metaurum flumen et Hasdrubal
   devictus et pulcher fugatis
     ille dies Latio tenebris,

qui primus alma risit adorea,
dirus per urbis Afer ut Italas
   ceu flamma per taedas vel Eurus
     per Siculas equitavit undas.

post hoc secundis usque laboribus
Romana pubes crevit, et impio
   vastata Poenorum tumultu
     fana deos habuere rectos,

dixitque tandem perfidus Hannibal
'cervi, luporum praeda rapacium,
   sectamur ultro, quos opimus
     fallere et effugere est triumphus.

gens, quae cremato fortis ab Ilio
iactata Tuscis aequoribus sacra
   natosque maturosque patres
     pertulit Ausonias ad urbis,

duris ut ilex tonsa bipennibus
nigrae feraci frondis in Algido,
   per damna, per caedis, ab ipso
     ducit opes animumque ferro.

Brave noble men father brave noble children.
In bulls and horses likewise the male's stamp shows
    Clearly; we never find
Fear bred from fierceness, eagles hatching doves.

Yet it is training that promotes the inborn
Talent, and morals that shore up the spirit.
    When laws of conduct fail,
Vice mars what nature once formed excellent.

How deep the debt you owe the clan of Nero,
Rome, the Metaurus witnesses, and routed
    Hasdrubal, and that day
When darkness lifted over Latium

And victory had its first fair Roman dawn since
The terrible African rode through our cities
    Like fire through pine-woods, like
An east wind whipping the Sicilian waves.

From that day Roman manhood plucked momentum
And marched from strength to strength. The shrines that
    Carthage
    Laid barbarously waste
Refurbished saw their gods stand straight again,

Till the perfidious Hannibal in despair cried,
'We are like deer, predestined prey, who yet would
    Run after ravening wolves.
Triumph for us lies in retreat and stealth.

This race that, risen undaunted from Troy's ashes,
Ferried its gods, old men and children over
    The tossing Tuscan sea
To house them safely in Italian towns,

Is like some tough-grained oak, lopped by the woodman
On Algidus, that dark-boughed, verdurous mountain:
    It bleeds, it feels the shock,
Yet draws in vigour from the very axe,

non hydra secto corpore firmior
vinci dolentem crevit in Herculem,
   monstrumve submisere Colchi
     maius Echioniaeve Thebae.

merses profundo: pulchrior evenit:
luctere: multa proruet integrum
   cum laude victorem geretque
     proelia coniugibus loquenda.

Carthagini iam non ego nuntios
mittam superbos: occidit, occidit
   spes omnis et fortuna nostri
     nominis Hasdrubale interempto.'

nil Claudiae non perficiunt manus,
quas et benigno numine Iuppiter
   defendit et curae sagaces
     expediunt per acuta belli.

V

Divis orte bonis, optime Romulae
custos gentis, abes iam nimium diu;
maturum reditum pollicitus patrum
   sancto concilio, redi.

lucem redde tuae, dux bone, patriae:
instar veris enim vultus ubi tuus
adfulsit populo, gratior it dies
   et soles melius nitent.

Flourishing as fiercely as the severed Hydra
Sprouted at chafing Hercules. Old Cadmus'
   Dragon-sown fields at Thebes
Never pushed up a prodigy like this.

Whelm it in water, it will come up brighter.
Throw it, and it will grapple with the winner
   Again and take the applause.
The wars they wage breed tales for wives to tell.

Henceforward I'll no more send home to Carthage
Arrogant messengers to proclaim my triumphs.
   Lost, lost all hope and sunk
Our nation's star now Hasdrubal is dead.'

There's not a feat that cannot be accomplished
By Claudian hands. Jupiter smiles upon their
   Works, and their wise designs
Pilot us through the rapids of our wars.

5

Great guardian of the race of Romulus
Born when the gods were being good to us,
   You have been absent now
   Too long. You pledged your word
   (The august Fathers heard)
To swift home-coming. Honour, then, that vow.

Restore, kind leader, to your countrymen
The light they lack. For, like the sunshine when
   It's springtime, where your face
   Lights on the people, there
   The weather turns to fair
And the day travels with a happier pace.

ut mater iuvenem, quem Notus invido
flatu Carpathii trans maris aequora
cunctantem spatio longius annuo
   dulci distinet a domo,

votis ominibusque et precibus vocat,
curvo nec faciem litore dimovet:
sic desideriis icta fidelibus
   quaerit patria Caesarem.

tutus bos etenim rura perambulat,
nutrit rura Ceres almaque Faustitas,
pacatum volitant per mare navitae,
   culpari metuit fides,

nullis polluitur casta domus stupris,
mos et lex maculosum edomuit nefas,
laudantur simili prole puerperae,
   culpam poena premit comes.

quis Parthum paveat, quis gelidum Scythen,
quis Germania quos horrida parturit
fetus, incolumni Caesare ? quis ferae
   bellum curet Hiberiae ?

condit quisque diem collibus in suis,
et vitem viduas ducit ad arbores;
hinc ad vina redit laetus et alteris
   te mensis adhibet deum;

te multa prece, te prosequitur mero
defuso pateris et Laribus tuum
miscet numen, uti Graecia Castoris
   et magni memor Herculis.

Picture a mother whose young son, detained
Beyond the sailing months by a cross-grained
   Southerly gale that sweeps
   The miles of Cretan foam,
   Winters away from home,
Sweet home; she calls for him, she keeps

Consulting omens, worrying the skies
With orisons and promises, her eyes
   Fixed on the curving shore.
   So does the motherland
   Keep loyal look-out and
Still miss the loved one she is waiting for.

When Caesar's here the ox plods safe and sound;
Ceres and gentle Plenty feed the ground
   With fruitfulness; across
   The uninfested seas
   Men speed with bird-like ease;
Honesty is afraid of its own loss;

No immoralities contaminate
Domestic faith, for custom and the State
   Have purged the taint of sin;
   Proud wives in children trace
   The true inherited face;
Crime hears the tread of Justice closing in.

Who fears the swarms that Germany brings forth
From her rough loins? Let Scythians in the north,
   Or Parthians rearm,
   Or the wild tribes of Spain
   Rally to war again,
We sleep as long as Caesar's safe from harm.

The husbandman on his own hillside sees
The day to bed, and gives his lonely trees
   In marriage to the vine.

'longas o utinam, dux bone, ferias
praestes Hesperiae!' dicimus integro
sicci mane die, dicimus uvidi,
    cum sol Oceano subest.

VI

Dive, quem proles Niobea magnae
vindicem linguae Tityosque raptor
sensit et Troiae prope victor altae
    Phthius Achilles,

ceteris maior, tibi miles impar,
filius quamvis Thetidis marinae
Dardanas turris quateret tremenda
    cuspide pugnax.

ille, mordaci velut icta ferro
pinus aut impulsa cupressus Euro,
procidit late posuitque collum in
    pulvere Teucro.

To supper thence he goes
Cheerfully, at the close
Of the first course inviting your divine

Assistance at his table. Wooed with prayers
And bowls of unmixed wine, your godhead shares
    His worship with the Lar
    That guards familial peace.
    Rome bows to you, as Greece
Did to great Hercules or Castor's star.

'Dear Emperor, long may you live to bless
Our Italy with holiday happiness!'
    Daily we raise the cry –
    At dawn before we've wet
    Our throats, and when the set
Sun's hidden in the sea and we're less dry.

6

O god whose power to avenge the tongue's presumption
Tityos the ravisher felt, and Niobe's children,
And, when tall Troy was almost his to enter,
    Phthian Achilles, he

Who had no peer in war yet could not match you,
Son though he was of the sea-goddess Thetis
And though his battle-rage made Ilium's towers
    Rock at his murderous spear.

A pine-tree reeling, bitten by the metal,
A cypress wrenched by the east wind and toppling
To earth, he fell; he lay sprawled out; he bowed his
    Neck in the Dardan dust.

ille non inclusus equo Minervae
sacra mentito male feriatos
Troas et laetam Priami choreis
   falleret aulam;

sed palam captis gravis, heu nefas! heu!
nescios fari pueros Achivis
ureret flammis, etiam latentem
   matris in alvo,

ni tuis victus Venerisque gratae
vocibus divum pater adnuisset
rebus Aeneae potiore ductos
   alite muros.

doctor argutae fidicen Thaliae,
Phoebe, qui Xantho lavis amne crines,
Dauniae defende decus Camenae,
   levis Agyieu.

spiritum Phoebus mihi, Phoebus artem
carminis nomenque dedit poetae.
virginum primae puerique claris
   patribus orti,

Deliae tutela deae fugaces
lyncas et cervos cohibentis arcu,
Lesbium servate pedem meique
pollicis ictum,

rite Latonae puerum canentes,
rite crescentem face Noctilucam,
prosperam frugum celeremque pronos
   volvere mensis.

nupta iam dices 'ego dis amicum,
saeculo festas referente luces,
reddidi carmen, docilis modorum
   vatis Horati.'

Would *he* have crouched inside the horse, that spurious
Peace-offering to Minerva, tricking Trojans
Into untimely holiday and carefree
    Dancing in Priam's court?

No, in fair fight he took and without pity
Slew; and indeed (O misery and horror!)
Would have roasted in Greek fire the speechless infants,
    Even the unborn babes,

Had not the father of the gods, won over
By your and lovely Venus's persuasion,
Nodded and pledged Aeneas other walls built
    Under more clement stars.

Lute-master, teacher of serene-voiced Thalia,
Who bathe your hair in Xanthus' water, smooth-cheeked
Lord of the noonday streets, Phoebus, uphold the
    Pride of my native Muse.

To you I owe my art, my inspiration:
You have conferred on me the name of poet.
Young girls of noble birth, young boys, the sons of
    Fathers of name and note,

Dear charges of the Delian archer-goddess
Whose shafts arrest the racing stags and lynxes,
Come, keep time to the Sapphic rhythm, keep the
    Beat of my plucking thumb,

Hymning Latona's son with all due honour,
Hymning the bright Night-shiner with her crescent
Torch, who makes ripe the crops and speeds the rapid
    Months of the rolling year.

One day, girl, when you marry, you shall tell them,
'When time brought round the great Centennial, I, too,
Trained in the measures of the poet Horace,
    Sang to the gods' delight.'

VII

Diffugere nives, redeunt iam gramina campis
    arboribusque comae;
mutat terra vices, et decrescentia ripas
    flumina praetereunt;
Gratia cum Nymphis geminisque sororibus audet
    ducere nuda choros.
immortalia ne speres, monet annus et almum
    quae rapit hora diem:
frigora mitescunt Zephyris, ver proterit aestas
    interitura simul
pomifer Autumnus fruges effuderit, et mox
    bruma recurrit iners.
damna tamen celeres reparant caelestia lunae:
    nos ubi decidimus
quo pater Aeneas, quo Tullus dives et Ancus,
    pulvis et umbra sumus.
quis scit an adiciant hodiernae crastina summae
    tempora di superi ?
cuncta manus avidas fugient heredis, amico
    quae dederis animo.
cum semel occideris et de te splendida Minos
    fecerit arbitria,
non, Torquate, genus, non te facundia, non te
    restituet pietas;
infernis neque enim tenebris Diana pudicum
    liberat Hippolytum,
nec Letheae valet Theseus abrumpere caro
    vincula Pirithoo.

Snow's gone away; green grass comes back to the meadows,
and green leaves
  Back to the trees, as the earth
Suffers her springtime change. Now last month's torrents,
diminished,
  Keep to their channels. The Grace
Dares to unrobe and, the Nymphs and her two sweet sisters
attending,
  Ventures a dance in the woods.
Yet be warned: each year gone round, each day-snatching
hour says,
  'Limit your hopes: you must die.'
Frost gives way to the warm west winds, soon summer shall
trample
  Spring and be trodden in turn
Under the march of exuberant, fruit-spilling autumn, then
back comes
  Winter to numb us again,
Moons make speed to repair their heavenly losses, but not so
  We, who, when once we have gone
Downwards to join rich Tullus and Ancus and father Aeneas,
  Crumble to shadow and dust.
Who knows whether the all-high gods intend an addition
  Made to the sum of today?
Give to your own dear self: that gift is the only possession
  Fingers of heirs cannot grasp.
Once you are dead, Torquatus, and Minos delivers his august
  Verdict upon your affairs,
No blue blood, no good deeds done, no eloquent pleading
  Ever shall conjure you back.
Great is the power of Diana and chaste was Hippolytus, yet
still
  Prisoned in darkness he lies.
Passionate Theseus was, yet could not shatter the chains
Death
  Forged for his Pirithous.

VIII

Donarem pateras grataque commodus,
Censorine, meis aera sodalibus,
donarem tripodas, praemia fortium
Graiorum, neque tu pessima munerum
ferres, divite me scilicet artium
quas aut Parrhasius protulit aut Scopas,
hic saxo, liquidis ille coloribus
sollers nunc hominem ponere, nunc deum.
sed non haec mihi vis, non tibi talium
res est aut animus deliciarum egens.
gaudes carminibus; carmina possumus
donare et pretium dicere muneri.
non incisa notis marmora publicis,
per quae spiritus et vita redit bonis
post mortem ducibus, non celeres fugae
reiectaeque retrorsum Hannibalis minae,
non incendia Carthaginis impiae
eius, qui domita nomen ab Africa
lucratus rediit, clarius indicant
laudes quam Calabrae Pierides: neque,
si chartae sileant quod bene feceris,
mercedem tuleris. quid foret Iliae
Mavortisque puer, si taciturnitas
obstaret meritis invida Romuli ?
ereptum Stygiis fluctibus Aeacum
virtus et favor et lingua potentium
vatum divitibus consecrat insulis.
dignum laude virum Musa vetat mori:
caelo Musa beat. sic Iovis interest
optatis epulis impiger Hercules,
clarum Tyndaridae sidus ab infimis
quassas eripiunt aequoribus ratis,
ornatus viridi tempora pampino
Liber vota bonos ducit ad exitus.

8

I'd dearly like to dedicate a present
To all my friends – libation bowls, or pleasant
Bronzes, or tripods such as in the arenas
Greek athletes won. In which case, Censorinus,
('Which case' assumes that I'm now rich and own
Something by Scopas hammered out of stone
Or else a portrait coloured by the running
Brush of Parrhasius – two masters cunning
In capturing god or hero to perfection),
You would receive the pick of the collection.
But I lack means, and you have ample store
Of works of art and can desire no more.
Poems you love, and these I *can* give, knowing
The proper value of what I'm bestowing.
Not marble cut with records, bringing breath
And spirit back to great men after death,
Not Hannibal's discomfort when he fled
Pell-mell, his threats recoiling on his head,
Not evil Carthage's last flames could throw
Such lustre round the elder Scipio,
Who brought the name of conquered Africa home,
As did the Muse of Ennius in Rome.
If history's pages leave them unrecorded,
Your deeds of merit cannot be rewarded.
The son of Mars and Ilia, Romulus –
Where would he stand today if envious
Silence had blocked fame's path? The power to wrest
Aeacus from Styx and place him in the Blest
Islands belongs to poets through the Muse's
Eloquence and affection. She refuses
To let the hero die. She can confer
Beatitude in heaven. By grace of her
Great Hercules, the tireless Labourer, sits
Feasting with Jove among the favourites.

IX

Ne forte credas interitura, quae
longe sonantem natus ad Aufidum
    non ante vulgatas per artis
        verba loquor socianda chordis:

non, si priores Maeonius tenet
sedes Homerus, Pindaricae latent
    Ceaeque et Alcaei minaces
        Stesichorive graves Camenae;

nec, si quid olim lusit Anacreon,
delevit aetas; spirat adhuc amor
    vivuntque commissi calores
        Aeoliae fidibus puellae.

non sola comptos arsit adulteri
crinis et aurum vestibus illitum
    mirata regalisque cultus
        et comites Helene Lacaena,

primusve Teucer tela Cydonio
direxit arcu; non semel Ilios
    vexata; non pugnavit ingens
        Idomeneus Sthenelusve solus

dicenda Musis proelia; non ferox
Hector vel acer Deiphobus gravis
    excepit ictus pro pudicis
        coniugibus puerisque primus.

Through her bright Castor with his star-twin saves
The vessel shattered in the trough of waves,
And Bacchus, with green vine crowning his hair,
Guides to a happy issue human prayer.

9

Born by far-booming Aufidus the poet, revolutionary the
    technique,
I have set my words to lyrical metres. Judge them.
Friend, should you be tempted to consider them short-lived,
Reconsider.
Maeonian Homer reigns supreme; true. But the music of
    Pindar and Simonides
Is not on that account inaudible,
Nor are angry Alcaeus or grave Stesichorus dumb.
Time has not demolished the trifles with which Anacreon
    amused himself.
Still to this day the flame flickers on
Of the passion the Aeolian girl whispered to her confidant,
    the lyre.
Do you think that Spartan Helen was unique among women
In adoring an adulterer's combed and curled hair, his gold-
    tissued robes, his princely pomp and retinue?
Was Teucer the first archer to shoot with a Cretan bow?
Were Sthenelus and huge Idomeneus the sole men in the
    world to fight battles worth a poet's commemoration?
Was one Troy only ever burnt?
When they bore hard blows for their chaste wives and
    children,
Fiery Deiphobus and ferocious Hector
Were doubtless doing what others had done before them.
Many brave men lived before Agamemnon,
But all went down unmourned, unhonoured into the
    smothering darkness
For lack of a minstrel to be their glory-giver.

vixere fortes ante Agamemnona
multi; sed omnes illacrimabiles
   urgentur ignotique longa
      nocte, carent quia vate sacro.

paulum sepultae distat inertiae
celata virtus. non ego te meis
   chartis inornatum sileri,
      totve tuos patiar labores

impune, Lolli, carpere lividas
obliviones. est animus tibi
   rerumque prudens et secundis
      temporibus dubiisque rectus,

vindex avarae fraudis et abstinens
ducentis ad se cuncta pecuniae,
   consulque non unius anni,
      sed quotiens bonus atque fidus

iudex honestum praetulit utili,
reiecit alto dona nocentium
   vultu, per obstantis catervas
      explicuit sua victor arma.

non possidentem multa vocaveris
recte beatum: rectius occupat
   nomen beati, qui deorum
      muneribus sapienter uti

duramque callet pauperiem pati
peiusque leto flagitium timet,
   non ille pro caris amicis
      aut patria timidus perire.

When courage lies hidden, it is little better off than shame
hushed up in the grave.
Lollius, I shall not leave your name without some lustre in my
verses,
Or let grey oblivion's envious jaws
Swallow your manifold exploits without my protest.
You have a mind that sees the world steadily: it keeps an
upright poise whatever the weather luck sends.
You bring the greedy profiteer to book, you stand unmoved
by that magnet of all things, money.
I salute you therefore as consul, not of one year only,
But of each day that you act as an honest judge, put honour
before advantage, dismiss the guilty briber with one cold
glance, and advance your standards into the thick of
corruption.
I do not call the millionaire the truly happy man.
He who has acquired the art of using the gifts of heaven
wisely
And of bearing difficult poverty in patience,
Who is more afraid of disgrace than death – he earns the title.
When it comes to dying for the sake of dear friends and
country,
That man does not pause.

X

O crudelis adhuc et Veneris muneribus potens,
insperata tuae cum veniet pluma superbiae,
et, quae nunc umeris involitant, deciderint comae,
nunc et qui color est puniceae flore prior rosae,
mutatus Ligurinum in faciem verterit hispidam,
dices 'heu' quotiens te speculo videris alterum,
'quae mens est hodie, cur eadem non puero fuit,
vel cur his animis incolumes non redeunt genae?'

XI

Est mihi nonum superantis annum
plenus Albani cadus; est in horto,
Phylli, nectendis apium coronis;
    est hederae vis

multa, qua crinis religata fulges;
ridet argento domus; ara castis
vincta verbenis avet immolato
    spargier agno;

cuncta festinat manus, huc et illuc
cursitant mixtae pueris puellae;
sordidum flammae trepidant rotantes
    vertice fumum.

10

Ah, Ligurinus,
Still cruel and swaggering with the gifts of Venus,
    The day's not far
When, stealing unawares, a beard will mar
    That debonair
Insouciance; that shoulder-rippling hair
    Fall; and the skin
Now pinker than the pinkest petal in
    A bed of roses
Suffer a rude and bristling metamorphosis.
    You'll say, 'Alas'
(Seeing the changed face in the looking-glass),
    'Why as a boy
Did I spurn the wisdom that I now enjoy?
    How now graft back
To wiser cheeks the rosiness they lack?'

11

I have a jar of Alban wine that musters
More than nine years; in my herb-beds
The parsley, Phyllis, clusters
To furnish for our heads
Green garlands; and luxuriant ivy spreads

To bind your hair with, make your beauty dazzle.
The house laughs bright with silver plate.
With laurel and with basil –
Chaste boughs – we decorate
The shrine that for the lamb can hardly wait.

All hands about the place are in a dither;
The boys, colliding with the girls,

ut tamen noris quibus advoceris
gaudiis, Idus tibi sunt agendae,
qui dies mensem Veneris marinae
    findit Aprilem,

iure sollemnis mihi sanctiorque
paene natali proprio, quod ex hac
luce Maecenas meus adfluentis
    ordinat annos.

Telephum, quem tu petis, occupavit
non tuae sortis iuvenem puella
dives et lasciva tenetque grata
    compede vinctum.

terret ambustus Phaethon avaras
spes, et exemplum grave praebet ales
Pegasus terrenum equitem gravatus
    Bellerophontem,

semper ut te digna sequare et ultra
quam licet sperare nefas putando
disparem vites. age iam, meorum
    finis amorum –

non enim posthac alia calebo
femina – condisce modos, amanda
voce quos reddas: minuentur atrae
    carmine curae.

Rush hither and run thither;
The toiling fire unfurls
The smoke and sends it up in sooty swirls.

But you must not be longer kept benighted
As to what joys today provides.
The feast you are invited
To celebrate divides
The month of sea-born Venus. On these Ides

A birthday falls, which rightly I judge nearly
More solemn and important than
My own. By this date, yearly,
Maecenas, that dear man,
Measures the passage of his mortal span.

Phyllis, you aim too hopefully above you,
For Telephus is hers by right
Of war. He'll never love you.
Her wealth and appetite
For kissing keep him handcuffed to delight.

Young Phaethon, who drove the sun one morning,
Fell scorched – which tells us to beware
Of greedy hopes. One more stern warning:
Winged Pegasus could not bear
Earth-born Bellerophon on him in the air.

Nature has set to human hope permitted
Limits which love should not transcend.
Then seek what you are fitted
To find – a well-matched friend.
Come, my last love – for here I reach the end

Of loving, and no woman shall excite me
Ever again – come, learn this air
And sing it to delight me.
A good song can repair
The ravages inflicted by black care.

XII

Iam veris comites, quae mare temperant,
impellunt animae lintea Thraciae;
iam nec prata rigent nec fluvii strepunt
    hiberna nive turgidi.

nidum ponit Ityn flebiliter gemens
infelix avis et Cecropiae domus
aeternum opprobrium, quod male barbaras
    regum est ulta libidines. ·

dicunt in tenero gramine pinguium
custodes ovium carmina fistula
delectantque deum cui pecus et nigri
    colles Arcadiae placent.

adduxere sitim tempora, Vergili;
sed pressum Calibus ducere Liberum
si gestis, iuvenum nobilium cliens,
    nardo vina merebere.

nardi parvus onyx eliciet cadum,
qui nunc Sulpiciis accubat horreis,
spes donare novas largus amaraque
    curarum eluere efficax.

ad quae si properas gaudia, cum tua
velox merce veni: non ego te meis
immunem meditor tingere poculis,
    plena dives ut in domo.

12

Those friends of spring, the Thracian gales,
Level the seas and swell the sails;
The hard clods thaw; the rivers flow
Quietly, without the melting snow
   That burdened them last month.

The luckless bird that cries and grieves
For Itys, builds now in the eaves.
She who the cruel lust of kings
Too barbarously avenged, still brings
   The house of Cecrops shame.

In the soft grass the boys who keep
A watch upon the fattening sheep
Pipe tunes, while Pan, who takes delight
In every flock and tree-dark height
   In Arcady, is pleased.

This season brings a thirst with it,
Virgil. But if you want to sit
With us, friend of young noblemen,
And drain wine pressed at Cales, then
   You'll have to pay your way.

One tiny nard-box earns as yours
A cask propped in Sulpicius' stores,
Bulging and brimming with the power
To give new hopes and drown the sour
   Savour of human care.

If you would like to join the spree,
Hurry – but bring your entrance fee.
I don't intend to dip your face
In wine scot-free, as if my place
   Were stocked like a rich man's.

verum pone moras et studium lucri,
nigrorumque memor, dum licet, ignium
misce stultitiam consiliis brevem:
    dulce est desipere in loco.

XIII

Audivere, Lyce, di mea vota, di
audivere, Lyce: fis anus, et tamen
    vis formosa videri
        ludisque et bibis impudens

et cantu tremulo pota Cupidinem
lentum sollicitas. ille virentis et
    doctae psallere Chiae
        pulchris excubat in genis.

importunus enim transvolat aridas
quercus et refugit te, quia luridi
    dentes te, quia rugae
        turpant et capitis nives.

nec Coae referunt iam tibi purpurae
nec cari lapides tempora quae semel
    notis condita fastis
        inclusit volucris dies.

quo fugit Venus, heu, quove color? decens
quo motus? quid habes illius, illius,
    quae spirabat amores,
        quae me surpuerat mihi,

felix post Cinaram notaque et artium
gratarum facies? sed Cinarae brevis
    annos fata dederunt,
        servatura diu parem

Then come at once and pause for breath
In chasing wealth. Remembering death
And death's dark fires, mix, while you may,
Method and madness, work and play.
    Folly is sweet, well-timed.

13

The gods have heard my prayer, Lyce, yes, it's heard and
      granted!
  You are old, Lyce. Yet, wanting to be wanted,
    You frolic shamelessly and drink
      Too much and, drunk, still think

That you can stir up sleepy Cupid with a shaking
  Serenade. But he's next door, awake in
    Chia's soft cheeks, whose youth and lyre
      Know how to rouse desire.

Relentless god, he never pauses in his flight
  To perch on withered oaks, and, catching sight
    Of your stained teeth and snow-white hair
      And wrinkles, veers elsewhere.

No purple silk from Cos, no shining precious stone
  Can restore the years now that the years have flown
    And Time has stored and locked away
      Stern records of each day.

Where is the fresh complexion now, the charm, the grace
  Of body that stole my self-command? What trace
    Is left of her who long ago
      Breathed love from head to toe,

Who, after Cinara, happily revelled in her place
  With that notoriously lovely face?
    The Fates dealt *her* an early grave,
      But you they plan to save

cornicis vetulae temporibus Lycen,
possent ut iuvenes visere fervidi
   multo non sine risu
      dilapsam in cineres facem.

XIV

Quae cura patrum quaeve Quiritium
plenis honorum muneribus tuas,
   Auguste, virtutes in aevum
      per titulos memoresque fastus

aeternet, o, qua sol habitabilis
illustrat oras, maxime principum?
   quem legis expertes Latinae
      Vindelici didicere nuper,

quid Marte posses. milite nam tuo
Drusus Genaunos, implacidum genus,
   Breunosque veloces et arces
      Alpibus impositas tremendis

deiecit acer plus vice simplici;
maior Neronum mox grave proelium
   commisit immanisque Raetos
      auspiciis pepulit secundis,

spectandus in certamine Martio,
devota morti pectora liberae
   quantis fatigaret ruinis,
      indomitus prope qualis undas

exercet Auster, Pleiadum choro
scindente nubes, impiger hostium
   vexare turmas et frementem
      mittere equum medios per ignis.

To linger on and on, Lyce, for years and years
   Like an old crow: a target for the jeers
     Of hot young rakes who'll come to gaze
       At the ash of beauty's blaze.

14

How shall a zealous parliament or people
With due emolument and ample honours
   Immortalise thy name
By inscription and commemorative page,

Augustus, O pre-eminent of princes
Wherever sunlight makes inhabitable
   The earth ? – O thou whose power
The Alpine tribes who lacked the Roman law

Learnt lately, when fierce Drusus with thy soldiers
Plucked the fleet Breuni down and the Genauni,
   Implacable mountaineers,
And, dealing double retribution, sent

Toppling their bastions on the fearful ledges.
Tiberius next moved into deadly action:
   Doomed by the Emperor's star,
The uncouth Rhaetians fled; Nero pursued,

A marvel and a prodigy in battle,
Carving vast havoc among hearts devoted
   To freedom and to death.
As tireless and determined as the wave-

Harrying south wind when the dancing Pleiads
Glimmer through ragged cloud, he shocked the enemy's
   Massed regiments, he spurred
His neighing charger through the holocaust.

sic tauriformis volvitur Aufidus,
qui regna Dauni praefluit Apuli,
   cum saevit horrendamque cultis
     diluviem meditatur agris,

ut barbarorum Claudius agmina
ferrata vasto diruit impetu
   primosque et extremos metendo
     stravit humum sine clade victor,

te copias, te consilium et tuos
praebente divos. nam tibi, quo die
   portus Alexandrea supplex
     et vacuam patefecit aulam,

fortuna lustro prospera tertio
belli secundos reddidit exitus,
   laudemque et optatum peractis
     imperiis decus arrogavit.

te Cantaber non ante domabilis
Medusque et Indus, te profugus Scythes
   miratur, o tutela praesens
     Italiae dominaeque Romae.

te, fontium qui celat origines,
Nilusque et Hister, te rapidus Tigris,
   te beluosus qui remotis
     obstrepit Oceanus Britannis,

te non paventis funera Galliae
duraeque tellus audit Hiberiae,
   te caede gaudentes Sygambri
     compositis venerantur armis.

As Aufidus, bull-throated and bull-headed,
Rampages through King Daunus's Apulia,
   Foaming and pondering
Huge inundation of the seeded fields,

So in his irresistible offensive
He broke the mail-clad columns of barbarians,
   And, scything van and rear,
Littered the ground with dead men not his own.

His was the victory, but thine the forces,
The strategy and the auspices of heaven.
   Just fifteen years ago
Suppliant Alexandria threw wide

Harbour and empty palace; now kind Fortune
Grants thee an anniversary achievement
   In arms, brings praise and adds
New longed-for lustres to thy high command.

The Mede, the Indian, the once unsubduable
Spaniard, the nomad Scythian – thee all nations
   (O shield of Italy
And her imperial metropolis)

Revere; thee Nile, who still conceals her secret
Springs, and the Danube and the hurrying Tigris
   And the whale-burdened sea
That bursts on the exotic British coast

Regard, and Gaul whose soldiers disregard death,
And obstinate Iberia. The Sygambri,
   Who love the sight of blood,
Pause at thy name and lay their weapons down.

XV

Phoebus volentem proelia me loqui
victas et urbis increpuit lyra,
    ne parva Tyrrhenum per aequor
      vela darem. tua, Caesar, aetas

fruges et agris rettulit uberes,
et signa nostro restituit Iovi
    derepta Parthorum superbis
      postibus et vacuum duellis

Ianum Quirini clausit et ordinem
rectum evaganti frena licentiae
    iniecit emovitque culpas
      et veteres revocavit artis,

per quas Latinum nomen et Italae
crevere vires, famaque et imperi
    porrecta maiestas ad ortus
      solis ab Hesperio cubili.

custode rerum Caesare non furor
civilis aut vis exiget otium,
    non ira, quae procudit ensis
      et miseras inimicat urbis.

non qui profundum Danuvium bibunt
edicta rumpent Iulia, non Getae,
    non Seres infidive Persae,
      non Tanain prope flumen orti.

nosque et profestis lucibus et sacris
inter iocosi munera Liberi
    cum prole matronisque nostris,
      rite deos prius apprecati,

15

Wars won and towns sacked – high were the themes I had
Planned; then Apollo twanged his rebuking lyre:
   'Stop! Little sails like yours should never
     Challenge the Tuscan, the epic ocean.'

Thy reign restores rich fruits to the countryside,
Augustus; brings back safe to our Capitol
   Crassus's long-lost standards, ripped from
     Arrogant Parthia's temple pillars;

Keeps Janus' arcade empty of warfare and
Shuts tight the gates there; bridles the runaway
   Beast, Licence, strayed far off the true road;
     Banishes vice and recalls the ancient

Rules whereby Rome's name, Italy's majesty,
Fame, strength and empire spread from the uttermost
   West, where the sun goes down at evening,
     East to the shores of his resurrection.

While Caesar stands guard, peace is assured, the peace
No power can break – not civil dissension or
   Brute force or wrath, that weapon-forger,
     Misery-maker for warring cities.

All men shall keep good faith with the Julian
Edicts: the Cossack born by the banks of Don,
   Wild Thracian, deep blue Danube drinker,
     Treacherous Parthian, distant Tartar.

We, too, for our part, workdays and holidays
Alike, among gay Bacchus's gifts to man,
   Prayer duly made where prayer is due, shall
     Gather the women and children round us

virtute functos more patrum duces
Lydia remixto carmine tibiis
   Troiamque et Anchisen et almae
   progeniem Veneris canemus.

And do as our forefathers did: Lydian
Pipe aiding voice, sing hymns to the heroes who
    Died well, to Troy, Anchises, kindly
        Venus and Venus's great descendants.

Q
HORATI
FLACCI
CARMEN
SAECULARE

HORACE
THE
CENTENNIAL
HYMN

Phoebe silvarumque potens Diana,
lucidum caeli decus, o colendi
semper et culti, date quae precamur
    tempore sacro,

quo Sibyllini monuere versus
virgines lectas puerosque castos
dis, quibus septem placuere colles,
    dicere carmen.

alme Sol, curru nitido diem qui
promis et celas aliusque et idem
nasceris, possis nihil urbe Roma
    visere maius.

rite maturos aperire partus
lenis, Ilithyia, tuere matres,
sive tu Lucina probas vocari
    seu Genitalis:

diva, producas subolem, patrumque
prosperes decreta super iugandis
feminis prolisque novae feraci
    lege marita,

certus undenos decies per annos
orbis ut cantus referatque ludos
ter die claro totiensque grata
    nocte frequentis.

vosque veraces cecinisse, Parcae,
quod semel dictum est stabilisque rerum
terminus servet, bona iam peractis
    iungite fata.

Diana, queen of forests, and Apollo,
O honoured and for ever to be honoured
Twin glories of the firmament, accord us
 All we beseech today –

Day of devotion, when the Sybil's verses
Enjoin the chaste, the chosen youths and maidens
To chant their hymns of worship to the patron
 Gods of our seven hills.

Kind sun, bright charioteer, bringer and hider
Of light, newborn each morning yet each morning
Unaltered, may thou never view a city
 Greater on earth than Rome.

Moon, gentle midwife, punctual in thy office,
Lucina, Ilithyia, Genitalis –
Be called whichever title is most pleasing –
 Care for our mothers' health.

Goddess, make strong our youth and bless the Senate's
Decrees rewarding parenthood and marriage,
That from the new laws Rome may reap a lavish
 Harvest of boys and girls

So that the destined cycle of eleven
Decades may bring again great throngs to witness
The games and singing: three bright days and three long
 Nights of the people's joy.

And you, O Fates, who have proved truthful prophets,
Your promise stands – and may time's sacred landmarks
Guard it immovably: to our accomplished
 Destiny add fresh strength.

fertilis frugum pecorisque tellus
spicea donet Cererem corona;
nutriant fetus et aquae salubres
    et Iovis aurae.

condito mitis placidusque telo
supplices audi pueros, Apollo;
siderum regina bicornis, audi,
    Luna, puellas:

Roma si vestrum est opus, Iliaeque
litus Etruscum tenuere turmae,
iussa pars mutare Lares et urbem
    sospite cursu,

cui per ardentem sine fraude Troiam
castus Aeneas patriae superstes
liberum munivit iter, daturus
    plura relictis:

di, probos mores docili iuventae,
di, senectuti placidae quietem,
Romulae genti date remque prolemque
    et decus omne.

quaeque vos bubus veneratur albis
clarus Anchisae Venerisque sanguis,
impetret, bellante prior, iacentem
    lenis in hostem.

iam mari terraque manus potentis
Medus Albanasque timet securis,
iam Scythae responsa petunt superbi
    nuper et Indi.

iam Fides et Pax et Honos Pudorque
priscus et neglecta redire Virtus
audet, apparetque beata pleno
    Copia cornu.

May Mother Earth, fruitful in crops and cattle,
Crown Ceres' forehead with a wreath of wheat-ears,
And dews and rains and breezes, God's good agents,
   Nourish whatever grows.

Sun-god, put by thy bow and deign to listen
Mildly and gently to the boys' entreaties.
Moon, crescent sovereign of the constellations,
   Answer the virgins' prayers.

Rome is your handiwork; in your safe-keeping
The Trojan band reached an Etruscan haven,
That remnant which, at your command, abandoned
   City and hearth to make

The auspicious voyage, those for whom pure-hearted
Aeneas, the last pillar of royal manhood
Left standing in burnt Troy, paved paths to greater
   Fame than they left behind.

Gods, by these tokens make our young quick pupils
Of virtue, give the aged peace and quiet,
Rain on the race of Romulus wealth, offspring,
   Honours of every kind;

And when, tonight, with blood of milk-white oxen
The glorious son of Venus and Anchises
Invokes you, grant his prayers. Long may Augustus
   Conquer but spare the foe.

Now Parthia fears the fist of Rome, the fasces
Potent on land and sea; now the once haughty
Ambassadors from the Caspian and the Indus
   Sue for a soft reply.

Now Faith and Peace and Honour and old-fashioned
Conscience and unremembered Virtue venture
To walk again, and with them blessed Plenty,
   Pouring her brimming horn.

augur et fulgente decorus arcu
Phoebus acceptusque novem Camenis,
qui salutari levat arte fessos
   corporis artus,

si Palatinas videt aequus aras,
remque Romanam Latiumque felix
alterum in lustrum meliusque semper
   proroget aevum.

quaeque Aventinum tenet Algidumque,
quindecim Diana preces virorum
curet et votis puerorum amicas
   applicet auris.

haec Iovem sentire deosque cunctos
spem bonam certamque domum reporto,
doctus et Phoebi chorus et Dianae
   dicere laudes.

Apollo, augur, bright-bowed archer, well-loved
Music-master of the nine Muses, healer
Whose skill in medicine can ease the body's
   Ills and infirmities,

By thy affection for the Palatine altars
Prolong, we pray, the Roman State and Latium's
Prosperity into future cycles, nobler
   Eras, for evermore.

Diana, keeper of the sacred hilltops
Of Aventine and Algidus, be gracious
To the prayers of the Fifteen Guardians, to the children
   Bend an attentíve ear.

That Jove and all the gods approve these wishes
We, the trained chorus, singers of the praises
Of Phoebus and Diana, carry homewards
   Happy, unshaken hope.

NOTES

BOOK ONE

Ode I

10 . . . three times public magistrate. The greatest success to which a Roman politician could aspire was to hold in one lifetime the curule aedileship (control of temples, buildings, markets and games), the praetorship (administration of justice), and the consulship (military command).

15 . . . an Attaline reward. The kings of Pergamus, especially Attalus III, were famous for their wealth.

18 . . . Cyprian. Cyprus, by virtue of its geographical position, played an important part in Mediterranean shipbuilding and trade.

46 . . . her sister Muse. Polyhymnia, who is referred to, was the Muse of sacred song, Euterpe of flute-playing.

47 . . . the Lesbian lyre. Lesbos was the home of Alcaeus and Sappho, the Greek lyric poets whom Horace regarded as his models.

Ode II

1–20 These lines describe the portents which terrified Rome after the murder of Julius Caesar.

14 . . . the Tuscan side. The right-hand side, since Etruria (Tuscany) was situated to the north of Rome.

15 . . . Vesta's temple and King Numa's palace. Numa (q.v.) built a temple to Vesta, goddess of the hearth, and a palace at the foot of the Palatine, which was on the east (left) side of the Tiber.

18 . . . avenger of . . . Ilia. Ilia (see also note to 3.iii. 30–32) became the wife of the river-god Tiber, into whose waters she was thrown by order of her uncle Amulius.

27 . . . the twelve Virgins. The Vestal Virgins guarded the fire of the goddess Vesta, symbol of Rome's eternity.

41 . . . winged boy of gentle Maia. The god Mercury.

44 . . . Caesar's avenger. Caesar here is Julius Caesar. In the last line of the ode 'Caesar' refers of course to Augustus himself.

Ode III

3 i.e. Castor and Pollux, protectors of seafarers.

9 . . . his Attic goal. We knew nothing of this voyage to Greece: Virgil's one recorded visit to Athens was at a later date, in b.c. 19.

Ode IV

5 . . . the Cytherean. i.e. Venus, who rose from the sea near the island of Cythera.

18 . . . rule the feast by dice-throw. It was customary among the ancients to elect a 'president' at feasts, whose main duty was to

choose the various wines and regulate the order in which they were
to be drunk and the proportion of water with which they were to be
diluted. Election was effected by dice.

Ode V

13–16 Sailors who survived shipwreck sometimes dedicated the clothes
they were rescued in to Neptune and commemorated this event on a
votive tablet.

Ode VI

9 . . . his savage pique. Achilles had been thwarted in his love for
Briseis (q.v.) and in anger withdrew from the siege of Troy.

12 . . . Pelops' house of blood. The story of Pelops (q.v.) and his descend-
ants, among whom were Agamemnon, Orestes and Electra, was a
popular theme for tragedians.

Ode VII

3 . . . haunt of Apollo. The god's oracular shrine was at Delphi.

12 . . . the Sibyl's booming grotto. Albunea, a prophetess, had a foun-
tain and grotto sacred to her at Tibur.

28–29 . . . Teucer founded the new Salamis in Cyprus.

Ode VIII

9 . . . the Tiber in flood. Military exercises took place on the Campus
Martius (q.v. under Mars) and often ended with a plunge in the
Tiber.

14–18 Achilles' mother, Thetis, is said to have dressed him in girl's
clothing so that he would avoid being called to fight at Troy, where
she knew he was destined to die.

Ode X

20–24 Referring to Priam's midnight visit to Achilles to recover the
body of his son Hector.

Ode XI

3 . . . Chaldees. The study of astronomy and astrology was especially
practised by the Chaldaeans.

Ode XII

23 . . . the Virgin. Diana, goddess of woodlands and hunting.

27 . . . Leda's twin sons. Castor and Pollux.

34 . . . fasces. See note to 3.ii.20.

35–36 Cato the Younger (q.v.) killed himself at Utica shortly after the
battle of Thapsus in B.C. 46, at which the senatorial or republican
party was crushed.

37 . . . Regulus. See note to 3.v.13.

NOTES

41–42 ... Fabricius, Camillus, Curius. All well-known figures from Rome's early history.

46 ... the Julian star. Referring to the descendants of Julius Caesar, among whom was Augustus.

49 ... son of Saturn. Jupiter.

Ode XIV

1 ... good ship. The ship of state.

14 ... Pontic pine. Pontus, a territory south of the Black Sea, was famous for its timber.

21 Horace is probably referring to his views at the time when he was a partisan of the republican party under Brutus.

Ode XV

2 ... his host's wife. Helen, wife of Menelaus.

20 ... the Ithacan. Ulysses.

34 ... Achilles' angry faction. See note to 1.vi.9.

Ode XVI

5 ... Pythian. Of Pytho, or Delphi, the seat of the god's oracle.

10 ... Noric. Noricum, a district in the Tyrol, was famous for its steel.

Ode XVII

27 ... one man. i.e. Ulysses. Circe, a sorceress, tried to detain him on her island from returning home to his wife, Penelope.

Ode XVIII

9 ... the Thracians. A race noted for their drunkenness.

13 ... Berecynthian horns. i.e. of the type used in the worship of Cybele (q.v.) on Mt. Berecynthus in Phrygia.

Ode XIX

2 ... Semele's son. Bacchus.

7 ... a Parian mine. Paros, an island in the Aegean, was noted for its white marble.

Ode XX

5–6 The illness of Maecenas and the applause that greeted him when he entered the theatre on his recovery are mentioned again in 2.xvii.

Ode XXVI

6 ... beneath the Bear. Especially referring to Dacia (q.v.), a country always feared by the Romans.

Ode XXVII

23–24 ... triple hell-hound. The Chimaera, a fire-breathing, triple-bodied monster, lion before, serpent behind, she-goat in the middle, who was overcome by Bellerophon (q.v.) riding the divine horse, Pegasus. Thereafter she was confined to the underworld.

Ode XXVIII

This ode has puzzled commentators. The generally accepted explanation is that it is a monologue spoken by the ghost of a drowned man whose body has been washed ashore near the tomb of Archytas (q.v.). The ghost first addresses Archytas, then calls to a passing sailor and asks for burial.

2–18 See under Pythagoras for an explanation of these lines.

25 . . . stormy Orion's friend. The constellation of Orion set in early November, usually a period of stormy weather.

29 . . . a few shifting grains. The ancients attached great importance to burial: the soul of an unburied body was condemned to wander on the shores of the Styx and not to be received into the underworld. Three handfuls of earth or sand constituted a legitimate burial.

Ode XXIX

2 . . . Arabian loot. An expedition was made into Arabia in B.C. 24. It was a failure.

Ode XXX

1 Praxiteles' famous statue of Venus was at Cnidos, a town on the coast of Caria in Asia Minor; Paphos, in Cyprus, was also associated with Venus: see note to 3.xxvi.

Ode XXXI

4 . . . Sardinian millionaires. Sardinia supplied Rome with corn, and like Calabria and Sicily was noted for its huge private estates.

12 . . . Tyre and Sidon. The great trading centres of the eastern Mediterranean.

Ode XXXII

7 . . . the Lesbian patriot. Alcaeus (q.v. under Lesbos).

Ode XXXV

1 . . . O goddess. Fortune, who had two statues at Antium, a town on the west coast of Italy a little south of Rome.

8 . . . Bithynian-timbered. See note to 1.xiv.14. Bithynia was situated directly to the west of Pontus.

29 . . . bound for Britain. Augustus proposed to visit Britain in B.C. 27; but his plans proved abortive.

34 . . . fratricides. A reference to the civil wars which had bedevilled recent Roman history.

Ode XXXVI

10 . . . changed the dark toga for the white. Roman children wore a purple-fringed toga. At about fifteen they exchanged this for the white *toga virilis*.

Ode XXXVII

3–4 . . . the priests of Mars. The Salii (q.v.). On special occasions the images of the gods were brought out into the street, placed on couches and served with a feast.

7 . . . the wild Queen. Cleopatra.

10 . . . half-men. Cleopatra's eunuch slaves.

12 . . . all her fleet burnt. In fact it was Antony's fleet that was burnt at Actium, while Cleopatra's fled.

BOOK TWO

Ode I

1 . . . Metellus. See under Pollio.

4 . . . doomed alliances of triumvirs. Ditto.

13 . . . the Attic buskin. On the Athenian stage tragic actors used to wear the cothurnus, a high-heeled boot, to give themselves added height and presence.

16 . . . Dalmatia's war. Pollio was accorded a triumph in B.C. 39 for his defeat of the Parthini.

21–24 This stanza probably describes the battle of Pharsalia, where Cato the Younger (q.v.) and Pompey opposed the Caesarians.

25–28 . . . reap their revenge. At the battle of Thapsus (B.C. 46) in North Africa the Pompeians and Cato were finally defeated with great loss. A century earlier, the Roman armies under P. Scipio Africanus had sacked Carthage, and later, in the Jugurthine wars ending with Jugurtha the Numidian king's death in B.C. 104, North Africa again saw many Roman victories.

Ode II

11 . . . the Carthaginians of both countries. Carthage had settlements directly to the north and south of the Straits of Gibraltar.

Ode III

15 Human life was represented in mythology as a thread being spun by the sister Fates, Clotho, Lachesis and Atropos. Death took place when the thread was cut by Atropos.

Ode IV

8 . . . the virgin. Cassandra, Priam's daughter.

Ode VI

11 . . . waging war. Horace had fought on the losing side at Philippi (q.v.).

14–15 The sheep were so valuable that they were given leather jackets to keep their fleeces clean.

Ode VII

7–9 After Philippi a large proportion of Brutus' supporters was pardoned by Octavian. The restoration of Pompeius' full civil rights may have been delayed because he continued for some time to support the beaten faction.

18 . . . by Mercury. A satirical imitation of Homer, who continually uses divinities to rescue his heroes from predicaments of combat.

31–33 See note to 1.iv.18.

Ode XII

2–3 Referring to the victories of Duilius at Mylae in B.C. 260 and of Lutatius Catulus off the Aegatian islands in B.C. 241.

Ode XIII

8 . . . Colchic poisons. Colchis, near the Black Sea, was the home of the sorceress Medea.

23 . . . judge of the dead. Aeacus. He was a just ruler on earth, and therefore made one of the three judges in Hades with Minos and Rhadamanthus.

24 . . . the Aeolian lyre. See note to 4.iii.14.

27 and 31 exile . . . and tyrants banished. Alcaeus himself was exiled from Lesbos for his opposition to the tyrant Myrsilus, who was later driven out.

34 . . . the hundred-headed Hell-dog. Cerberus.

37–38 . . . the sire of Pelops. Tantalus (q.v.).

Ode XV

4 . . . bachelor plane-trees. Vines were usually trained upon (wedded to) elms. Plane-trees were useless for this purpose.

17–18 . . . the turf by the roadside. Used for roofing cottages.

Ode XVI

9 . . . a consul's rodded lictors. See note to 3.ii.20.

Ode XVII

24 . . . rescued you. Maecenas' illness and recovery are also mentioned in 1.xx.

NOTES

Ode XVIII

5–6 Attalus III, King of Pergamus, unexpectedly bequeathed his property to the Roman people in B.C. 133.

35 . . . Hell's ferryman. Charon (q.v.).

Ode XIX

11 . . . unchainer of the mind. One of Bacchus' titles was Liber, 'the liberator'.

19 . . . your radiant bride. Ariadne.

22–23 Pentheus, king of Thebes, opposed the worship of Bacchus. He was killed by the god's followers and his palace was overthrown by an earthquake.

24 Lycurgus, who also opposed the god's entry into his territory, was punished by madness and death.

31 . . . the brigade of Giants. See under Giants.

Ode XX

16 . . . Hyperborean lands. A vague region to the north of the known world.

BOOK THREE

Ode I

10 . . . Field of Mars. The Campus Martius (q.v. Mars) was the exercise ground of the army, and was also used as a civic assembly ground at elections. It lay low and the rich lived on the hills: hence 'descend'.

13 . . . mob of clients. The term 'client' signified a dependent on a person of high rank or wealth. In its original form the relationship was one of mutual regard and benefit, one party providing services, the other patronage. With increasing wealth and the break-up of the close-knit Roman society under the Empire clients became mere hangers-on, despised and given small dole by status-seeking patrons.

17–18 Referring to the feast of Damocles, a court flatterer during the tyranny of Dionysius I of Syracuse. The tyrant, on being called the happiest of men by Damocles, invited him to partake of the sort of happiness found by a monarch; the invitation was to a dinner with the guest seated directly underneath a sword suspended by a single horse-hair.

28 . . . the Kid . . . Arcturus. Constellations that rise and set respectively in early and later October.

Ode II

20 . . . fasces. Bundles of wooden rods bound together with an axe enclosed, symbols of authority carried by the lictors in front of consuls and certain other officials on ceremonial occasions.

27 The mysteries, or rituals, connected with the worship of the corn-goddess Ceres, whom the Romans identified with the Greek Demeter, were supposed to be kept secret by the initiated.

Ode III

9–10 . . . Hercules and Pollux: frequently taken as examples of deified mortals or demigods.

13–14 According to legends, Bacchus visited mankind to teach the use of the vine and civilisation. This is symbolised by the taming of tigers, who drew his chariot in triumphal progress through Asia.

15–16 Having founded and become the first king of Rome, Romulus is said to have disappeared in a thunderstorm in a chariot drawn by the horses of Mars, his father.

19 . . . a fatal arbiter. Paris, who in his famous judgment rejected Hera and Athene in favour of Aphrodite.

20 . . . a foreign whore. Helen, the wife of Menelaus the Spartan, who was carried off to Troy by Paris, thus provoking the Trojan war.

24 Laomedon, a previous king of Troy, employed Apollo and Poseidon to build the city walls and then refused them payment.

30–32 Mars was the father of Romulus by Rhea Silvia, here identified with Ilia, Aeneas' daughter and a Trojan priestess. The speaker, Juno, was the mother of Mars.

60 There appear to have been rumours current in Rome that Augustus might move the seat of government from Rome to the East.

Ode IV

27–29 Horace mentions his escape from a falling tree in 2.xiii and 3.viii, but makes no other mention of nearly being shipwrecked.

33 The inhabitants of Britain had a reputation for cruelty throughout the ancient world, probably on account of the Druids.

37–38 Refers either to billeting the troops in winter quarters or to settling veterans in towns at the close of a campaign.

50 . . . the brothers. Otus and Ephialtes, who tried to build a staircase to heaven.

53–56 Mimas and the others mentioned in this stanza were all Giants (q.v.).

73–76 The eruptions of Etna and other volcanoes were explained as the result of the struggles of the Giants (q.v.) to escape from their earthly prisons.

80 Pirithous attempted to abduct the goddess Proserpine from Hades.

Ode V

5 A Roman army under Crassus was destroyed at Carrhae in northern Mesopotamia by the Parthians in B.C. 53. The survivors, who were taken prisoner, settled among the 'barbarians'.

NOTES

10 ... the Sacred Shields. These were kept by the Salii, the priests of Mars, and were a symbol of the stability of the Empire.

13 Regulus and his army were defeated by the Carthaginians in B.C. 256 and he and many of his men taken prisoner. In B.C. 250 he was released and sent back to Rome to arrange a peace, on condition that, if he failed, he was to return to captivity. Regulus advised Rome to continue the war, returned to Carthage and was tortured and put to death with the rest of his soldiers.

18 ... eagles. The carved eagles on the standards of the legions.

Ode VI

9 Monaeses and Pacorus were both Parthian generals. The latter defeated a Roman army in B.C. 40: Monaeses' victory is otherwise unrecorded.

15 At Actium Dacian bowmen fought against Octavian under Antony, alongside Cleopatra's Egyptian troops.

Ode VII

5 ... the tempestuous Goat. A constellation that rises at the end of September.

Ode VIII

1 ... Matrons' Day. The Matronalia was a festival celebrated by married women in honour of Juno in her role as goddess of child-birth.

6 ... in both tongues. i.e. Greek and Latin.

11 ... Tullus' consulship. A Tullus was consul in both B.C. 66 and 33.

12 ... the upstairs niche. The Romans stored wine in the *apotheca* at the top of the house, because the smoke from the fire was thought to help to mellow it.

Ode XI

13–24 This passage refers to the legendary exploits of the musician Orpheus, who rescued his wife Eurydice from Hades.

24 ... Danaids. The daughters of Danaus (q.v.).

Ode XIV

1–5 Augustus returned from his Spanish campaign in B.C. 25. Line 3 may refer to the serious illness he contracted in the course of it.

10 ... our leader's sister. Octavia, the widow of Antony.

23 The Marsian war (B.C. 90–88) was fought between the Italian allies (of whom the Marsians were reputedly the bravest soldiers) and Rome, over the question of franchise. Although the war was not conclusive, full Roman citizenship was later granted to all the Italians.

Ode XVI

1–8 Acrisius, king of Argos, was told by an oracle that the son of his daughter Danae would kill him. He therefore confined Danae in a locked tower; but Zeus, her lover, turned himself into a shower of gold and so succeeded in visiting her. Their son, Perseus, later killed Acrisius accidentally in a discus-throwing competition.

11 . . . the Argive augur. Amphiaraus, who was persuaded by his wife to take part in the expedition of the Seven against Thebes, which he knew would end in disaster; she in her turn had been bribed to do this by Polynices, the rightful king of Thebes, on whose behalf the expedition was taking place.

13 . . . the man from Macedon. Philip II, father of Alexander the Great, who gained possession of numerous Greek cities by bribery.

15 . . . tough naval captains. Horace may be thinking of Menas, an admiral who twice changed sides during the struggle between Octavian and Augustus.

18 . . . yet still a knight. Maecenas consistently refused to hold any office or claim senatorial rank and remained a member of the equestrian order.

Ode XVII

1–4 L. Aelius Lamia (q.v.), to whom this ode is addressed, probably claimed to be descended from the hero Lamus mentioned in Homer's *Odyssey*.

Ode XVIII

8–22 The annual festival in honour of Faunus (the Faunalia) took place in early December.

Ode XIX

The ode begins as if the feast in honour of Murena were still being arranged, but in line 12, by an imaginative transition, Horace pictures it as in progress.

22 . . . the Phrygian flute. It was in Phrygia that the goddess Cybele was worshipped: flute music played an important part in the orgiastic rites.

Ode XX

19–20 . . . the boy . . . Jove kidnapped. Ganymede, who became his cup-bearer.

Ode XXI

8 . . . from upstairs. See note to 3.viii.12.

Ode XXII

2 . . . goddess of three shapes and faces. In heaven Luna, on earth Diana the huntress, in the underworld Hecate. Although Diana was the patroness of chastity, she shared with Juno the role of presider over childbirth. See the Centennial Hymn, lines 13–16.

Ode XXIII

14 . . . hecatombs: The term once meant the sacrifice of a hundred oxen, but later was applied to any large-scale sacrifice of animals.
20 A mixture of parched meal and salt, according to Pliny, was offered by those who could not afford incense.

Ode XXIV

55 . . . Greek hoops. The theme of the vicious, effeminate Greek constantly recurs in Roman literature.

Ode XXV

9 . . . the wild reveller. The worshipper of Bacchus who has 'followed the god' all night across country.

Ode XXVI

6 and 13 Venus, according to legend, sprang from the sea and first landed at Paphos in Cyprus. Her cult was prevalent all over the Mediterranean. One of her many temples was at Memphis in Egypt.

Ode XXVII

15 . . . darting leftwards. In augury the left was the unlucky side. The Roman augurs faced south, the Greeks north, when taking observations. To the Romans, therefore, good omens came from the eastern sky.
42 . . . the Ivory Gate. According to Homer, dreams to be accomplished come upon the sleeper through a gate of horn, baseless ones through a gate of ivory.

Ode XXVIII

2–3 The festival of Neptune was celebrated on July 23rd.
22–25 Referring to Venus, whose chariot was drawn by swans.

Ode XXIX

17–18 . . . Cepheus, Procyon and Leo. All these stars rise in July.
22 . . . the shaggy wood-god. Silvanus.
64 . . . the Heavenly Twins. Castor and Pollux, protectors of seafarers.

BOOK FOUR

Ode I

41–42 See note to 1.viii.9 for the customary bathe in the Tiber after exercises on the Campus Martius.

Ode II

3–4 The Icarian Sea, in the eastern Aegean, was named after Icarus (q.v.), the son of Daedalus, who was drowned there.

11 . . . dithyrambs. Greek choral odes, originally sung in honour of
Dionysus (Bacchus). Pindar's were written in exceptionally free verse,
and contained frequent neologisms and audacious transitions.

35–36 The Sygambri were a German tribe who gained a victory over
a Roman army in B.C. 16, but sought peace when they heard Augus-
tus himself was marching against them. The Via Sacra, the principal
street in Rome, was where the triumphal processions took place.

44 The law-courts were in the Forum and were closed on occasions of
public rejoicing.

Ode III

4 . . . the Isthmus. The Isthmian Games were celebrated on the
Isthmus of Corinth every other year.

14 . . . Aeolian. The dialect used by the lyric poets Alcaeus and
Sappho.

19 . . . the sacred well. i.e. in Pieria (q.v.).

20 . . . the golden shell. The lyre was made of tortoise-shell.

Ode IV

17–18 Drusus and Tiberius (later Emperor), Augustus' two step-sons,
defeated the Rhaeti and Vindelici, Tyrolean tribes, in B.C. 15.

28 . . . two boys. Drusus and Tiberius.

37–40 Referring to the consul C. Claudius Nero's defeat of Hasdrubal,
Hannibal's brother, at the river Metaurus in north-east Italy in B.C.
207.

42 . . . the terrible African. Hannibal.

74 . . . Claudian hands. The Claudian family was bound up with the
Julian, from which Augustus came.

Ode V

1 . . . Great guardian. Augustus.

5 . . . the august Fathers. The Senate.

31–36 Augustus had enacted severe laws against adultery.

51–54 The worship of Augustus as a demigod was encouraged. The
Senate had decreed that libations should be poured to him at private
as well as public banquets.

Ode VI

12 . . . Dardan. Trojan.

35 . . . Sapphic rhythm. See under Lesbos.

42 . . . Centennial. In B.C. 17 Augustus reinstituted the so-called
Secular Games, a festival celebrating the preservation of the State
and supposed to be held once in every 110 years. On the third and
last day of the games an ode was sung in Apollo's temple by a choir
of boys and girls, and it was Horace who was commissioned to write
it. See the Centennial Hymn.

NOTES

Ode VII

15 . . . Tullus and Ancus. Legendary kings of Rome.

Ode VIII

19–20 Horace wrongly ascribes the burning of Carthage to the elder Scipio. Consequently some editors have argued that this passage is either corrupt or not the work of Horace.

Ode IX

10 . . . the Aeolian girl. Sappho.

Ode XI

20 . . . these Ides. i.e. April 13. April was sacred to Venus.

Ode XII

6 . . . the luckless bird. Either the swallow or the nightingale. The story goes that Tereus, king of Athens, married to Procne, ravished her sister Philomela. In revenge Procne served up her son Itys' flesh for Tereus to eat. The two sisters were thereupon turned into a nightingale and a swallow, but the legends vary as to which became which.

17 . . . Virgil. Almost certainly not the poet.

22 . . . Sulpicius' stores. Warehouses on the banks of the Tiber.

Ode XIV

8–32 For Drusus' and Tiberius' (also called Nero) German campaign, see note to 4.iv.17–18.

35 . . . fifteen years ago. In B.C. 30, after Antony and Cleopatra's defeat at Actium.

50 . . . the Sygambri. See note to 4.ii.35–36.

Ode XV

7 . . . Crassus's long-lost standards. See note to 3.v.5.

9–10 . . . Janus' arcade . . . shuts tight. This was a well-known arcade in Rome with two entrances, which were kept open in time of war and closed in time of peace.

32 . . . Venus's great descendants. The Roman people, who thought of themselves as descended from the Trojans who escaped from Troy and came to Italy under Aeneas, the son of Venus and Anchises.

THE CENTENNIAL HYMN

For an account of the Centennial Festival, see note to 4.vi.42.

14 The three names exemplify the Moon-goddess's role as presider over childbirth. Lucina was also Juno's name in this capacity; Ilithyia was a Greek goddess of childbirth; Genitalis, 'She who brings to birth', is a title not found elsewhere.

21 . . . the destined cycle of eleven decades. See note to 4.vi.42.

50 . . . the glorious son of Venus and Anchises. Augustus, who was their descendant according to Roman tradition.

53 . . . fasces. See note to 3.ii.20.

71 . . . the Fifteen Guardians. The keepers of the Sibylline Books, who had charge of the Centennial Festival.

GLOSSARY

Achaemenes: founder of Persia's first royal house, and ancestor of Cyrus.

Acherontia: a small town in Apulia.

Aeacus: son of Zeus: his family tree downwards included Peleus (q.v.), Achilles and Neoptolemus. After his death he became one of the judges of the dead.

Aefula: a town in Latium.

Agamemnon: son of Atreus (q.v.), and leader of the Greek army at Troy.

Agrippa, M. Vipsanius: Augustus' war minister.

Ajax: (i) 'the Greater': son of Telamon (ii) 'the Lesser': son of Oileus. Both took part in the Trojan war.

Alban: the Alban lake was about fifty miles south-east of Rome. The district produced a wine second only to Falernian.

Alcaeus, Alcaic: see under Lesbos.

Algidus: a mountain in Latium.

Alyattes: son of Croesus, of proverbial wealth; king of Lydia.

Amphion: builder of Thebes: the sound of his lyre made the stones come together of their own accord.

Anacreon: a Greek lyric poet, who flourished in the sixth century B.C.

Anchises: a member of the royal house of Troy. Venus loved him and by him bore Aeneas.

Anio: a river that flows near Tibur (q.v.).

Antilochus: Nestor's son (q.v.), killed in the Trojan war.

Antiochus: Antiochus III, 'the Great', conquered most of Asia Minor, but was defeated in B.C. 190 by Scipio Africanus.

Apollo (Phoebus): god of the sun, and patron of poetry and the Muses.

Apulia: a wild district in the south-east of Italy.

Archytas: a mathematician of the Pythagorean school, who lived at Tarentum about B.C. 400.

Argos: a territory south of Corinth.

Athene (Pallas): the patron goddess of Athens, identified by the Romans with Minerva.

Atlas: a Giant who, for his part in the rebellion of the Titans against the gods, was condemned to support the heavens on his hands and neck. He was said to stand somewhere west of the Straits of Gibraltar.

Atreus: the legend of the House of Atreus was a favourite subject of the classical poets. The curse laid upon it by Thyestes (q.v.) was not worked out until the fourth generation.

Aufidus: a river in Apulia.

Augustus: the title assumed by Octavian when he became Emperor. See under Caesar.

Aulon: a valley near Tarentum (q.v.).

Aurora: the dawn goddess: see Tithonus.

Aventine: one of the Seven Hills of Rome.

Bacchus (Dionysus): god of wine.

Baiae: a favoured resort in the Bay of Naples.

Bandusia: a fountain either near Venusia (q.v.) or Tibur (q.v.).

Bantia: a town in Apulia.

Bellerophon: while he was a guest at the court of Proetus, king of Argos, Anteia, his host's wife, fell in love with him. He refused her advances, whereupon she reported to Proetus that he had assaulted her. Proetus attempted to have Bellerophon killed by having him sent against the Chimaera (q.v.), but he survived with the aid of the divine horse, Pegasus.

Bibulus, M. Calpurnius: consul in B.C. 59. His name, in the context in which it appears, carries alcoholic associations.

Bistonians: a Thracian tribe.

Bithynia: a territory lying to the west of Pontus (q.v.).

Briseis: a beautiful slave-girl, loved by Achilles. Agamemnon (q.v.) insisted on having her for himself, whereupon Achilles retired from the fighting-line to sulk in his tent.

Brutus, Marcus: leader of the republican opposition, who assassinated Julius Caesar and was killed at Philippi (q.v.).

Cadmus: founder of Thebes. By advice of Athene he sowed a field with dragon's teeth, which produced a harvest of armed men.

Caecuban: a local wine from Latium.

Caesar: the first Emperor of Rome, under whose rule Horace lived. Also called Octavian and Augustus.

Calabria: a district situated in the south-east, the 'heel', of Italy.

Cales: a town in Campania, a wine-producing area.

Calliope: the Muse of epic poetry.

Cantabri: a warlike tribe in north-western Spain.

Capitol: the south-west summit of the Capitoline, one of the Seven Hills of Rome, on which was erected the temple of Jupiter, Rome's special guardian.

Catilus: father of three sons who founded Tibur.

Cato, M. Porcius: (i) 'The Censor', an office he held in B.C. 184. He was famous for his austere and old-fashioned way of life, and for his attempts to force this discipline on others.
(ii) 'The Younger', great-grandson of the above. He fought with Pompey against Julius Caesar in the Civil Wars, and killed himself shortly after his side's defeat at Thapsus.

Cecrops: legendary first king of Athens.

Censorinus: consul in B.C. 8.

Centaurs: a legendary Thracian race with horses' hindquarters and men's torsos. See under Lapiths.

Cerberus: the monstrous three-headed (or by some accounts hundred-headed) dog that guarded the entrance to the underworld.

Ceres (Demeter): goddess of corn and harvest, mother of Proserpine.

Charon: the boatman of the underworld, who rowed dead souls across the Styx so that they could be received into Hades.

Chimaera: see note to 1.xxvii. 23.

Chios: an island in the Aegean, from which Rome imported wine.

Clio: the Muse of history.

Cocytus: one of the rivers of the underworld.

Codrus: the last king of Athens.

Concani: a tribe in north-western Spain.

Corybantes: the priests of the goddess Cybele (q.v.).

Cos: an island in the Aegean.

Cotiso: defeated by Crassus in B.C. 30.

Cragus: a mountain in Lycia (q.v.).

Crispus, C. Sallustius: grand-nephew and adopted son of the historian Sallust. He was a friend of Augustus, but held aloof from public office.

Cybele: an Asiatic goddess, whose followers were noted for their frenzied rites.

Cyclades: a group of small islands round Delos, in the Aegean.

Cyclops: one-eyed monsters who worked under Vulcan and forged Jove's thunderbolts in Mount Etna.

Cynthia: another name for Diana.

Cyrus: in the sixth century B.C. head of the Persian royal house, from whom the Parthians claimed descent.

Daedalus: see under Icarus.

Danaus: the mythical founder of Argos and father of fifty daughters. His brother Aegyptus had fifty sons, and these pursued Danaus and his family to Argos. Danaus was compelled to consent to his daughters marrying Aegyptus' sons, but ordered them to kill their husbands on their wedding night. This they all did with one exception. The forty-nine guilty brides were condemned in Hades perpetually to try to fill leaking jars with water.

Daunus: a legendary king of Apulia.

Deiphobus: a Trojan warrior, Hector's brother.

Delos: an island in the Aegean, Apollo's birthplace.

Diana (Artemis): goddess of hunting.

Diomede: leader of the men of Argos at the siege of Troy.

Dirce: a fountain near Thebes, near where Pindar (q.v.) was born.

Ennius: an early Roman epic poet (B.C. 239–169), and friend of the elder Scipio (q.v.).

Epirus: a territory to the north-west of Greece, off which the present Corfu lies.

Erymanthus: a mountain in Arcadia.

Eryx: a mountain in Sicily, where stood a temple of Aphrodite.

Europa: daughter of Agenor, king of Tyre. Zeus fell in love with her and, in the guise of a white bull, carried her off on his back over the sea to Crete.

Falernian: a strong and highly prized wine from Falernus in Campania.

Faunus: an Italian god of the countryside.

Forentum: a town in Apulia.

Formiae: a town in Latium, that gave its name to an excellent wine.

Gades: the modern Cadiz.

Gaetulia: a North African territory adjoining Numidia (q.v.).

Galaesus: a river near Tarentum.

Ganymede: Zeus's cup-bearer, renowned for his beauty. He was carried forcibly to heaven by the god's eagle.

Garganus: a mountain in Apulia.

Geloni: a nomadic Scythian tribe.

Geryon: one of the Giants (q.v.), who had three bodies and whose oxen were stolen by Hercules.

Getae: a Thracian tribe.

Giants: sons of Ge (Earth), often confused with the Titans (see under Atlas), who rose against the gods, were defeated, and punished by imprisonment under their mother Earth.

Graces: the three Graces, daughters of Zeus, were Aglaia, Thalia and Euphrosyne.

Gyas: a Giant (q.v.).

Hadria: the Adriatic Sea.

Hebrus: a Thracian river.

Hercules: a hero, famous for the twelve labours which he successfully accomplished.

Hesperus: the evening star.

Hippolyte: see under Peleus.

Hippolytus: killed on the orders of Phaedra, his stepmother, because he refused her advances, being devoted to chastity.

Hyades: a group of stars whose appearance indicated rough weather.

Hydaspes: a tributary of the Indus.

Hydra: a many-headed monster, which Hercules slew as one of his labours. Its heads grew again as soon as they were hacked off.

Hymettus: a mountain in Attica, still famous for its honey.

Iberia: Spain.

Icaros: a rocky island near Samos.

Icarus: the son of Daedalus, the mythical craftsman and inventor. Imprisoned on the island of Crete by Minos (q.v.), he and his father attached wings to their shoulders with wax, and flew away. Daedalus succeeded in his flight, but Icarus flew too near the sun, so that the wax melted and he fell into the sea and was drowned.

Iccius: a provincial administrator under Agrippa (q.v.), otherwise unknown.

Ida: a mountain near Troy.

Idomeneus: a Cretan warrior who fought for the Greeks at Troy.

Ilia: see note to 3.iii.30–32.

Ilium: a name of Troy.

Illyria: the country bordering on the Adriatic Sea, opposite Italy; now part of Yugoslavia.

Inachus: the legendary first king of Argos.

Itys: see note to 4.xii.6.

Ixion: tied to an ever-turning wheel in Hades, as a punishment for wooing Hera, Zeus's wife.

Julus: Julus Antonius, son of Antony, obtained the favour of Augustus and was made consul in B.C. 10. He is said to have written an epic poem.

Juno (Hera): queen of heaven and wife of Jupiter.

Jupiter (Zeus): father and ruler of the gods.

Lamia, L. Aelius: an aristocrat, Prefect of the City in A.D. 32.

Lanuvium: a town on a hill near the Appian Way.

Laomedon: see note to 3.iii.24.

Lapiths: a Thracian tribe who fought against and defeated the Centaurs (q.v.) in a battle provoked by the Centaurs' drunken behaviour at the Lapith king's wedding.

Lars (Lares): gods of the home and hearth.

Larissa: a city in Thessaly.

Latium: the district in Italy where Rome was situated.

Latona: mother, by Jupiter, of Apollo and Diana, also known as Leto.

Lesbos: an island in the Aegean, home of the lyric poets Terpander, Alcaeus and Sappho. The two latter gave their names to metres used extensively by Horace in the Odes. The Romans imported wine from Lesbos.

Leto: see under Latona.

Liber: a name of Bacchus, god of wine, 'the liberator'.

Liburnians: an Illyrian tribe, whose light galleys played a part in Octavian's victory at Actium.

Licinius, Lucius: Maecenas' brother-in-law, consul in B.C. 23 and brother of Proculeius (q.v.).

Licymnia: probably a pesudonym for Terentia, wife of Maecenas.

Lipara: an island off the coast of Sicily.

Liris: a river in Latium (q.v.).

Livia: the wife of Augustus.

Locris: a coastal district, opposite the island of Euboea.

Lollius, Marcus: consul in B.C. 21, highly regarded by Augustus.

Luceria: a town in Apulia.

Lucretilis: a mountain near Horace's farm at Tibur (q.v.).

Lucrinus: a lake near Naples.

Lycaeus: a mountain in Arcadia.

Lycia: a territory in Asia Minor, south of Troy; the Lycians sent troops to defend Troy against the Greeks.

Maecenas, Gaius: Augustus' trusted friend, and the patron of a large literary circle including Virgil and Horace.

Maeonia: an ancient name of Lydia.

Maia: the mother of Mercury by Zeus.

Manlius, L. Torquatus: consul in B.C. 65.

Marcelli: an aristocratic Roman family. A Marcellus became Augustus' son-in-law.

Marica: a local goddess worshipped in the marshlands at the mouth of the Liris.

Mars: god of war: the Field of Mars, or Campus Martius, was a large flat space bounded by the Tiber to the north-west of Rome.

Marsi: a central Italian tribe, noted as soldiers.

Massic: a wine of the same type as Falernian (q.v.).

Matinum: a coastal district in Apulia.

Melpomene: strictly the Muse of tragedy and dirges; sometimes the Muse of poetry in general.

Mercury (Hermes): messenger of the gods, patron of travellers and thieves.

Meriones: a Cretan charioteer at the siege of Troy.

Minerva: goddess of war and domestic crafts, identified by the Romans with Athene.

Minos: a legendary king of Crete, son of Zeus, and one of the three judges in the underworld.

Mitylene: a city on the island of Lesbos.

Murena: another name of L. Licinius (q.v.).

Mycenae: a city in Argos.

Myrmidons: a warlike race from Thessaly, who accompanied Achilles to the Trojan war.

Naiades: the river-nymphs.

Neptune (Poseidon): god of the sea.

Nereides: the sea-nymphs.

Nereus: a sea-god.

Nestor: king of Pylos: he played an important role in the Greek campaign at Troy as adviser and elder statesman.

Niobe: daughter of Tantalus (q.v.) and mother of seven sons and seven daughters, who dared to boast of her superiority over Latona. As a punishment, all her children were killed by Apollo and Diana, Latona's children.

Nireus: spoken of by Homer as the most beautiful of the Greeks.

Numa: successor to Romulus (q.v.) as king of Rome.

Numantia: a town in Spain, captured by P. Scipio Africanus in B.C. 133 after having been besieged for eight years.

Numidia: a country lying south and west of Carthage, in Horace's youth ruled by King Juba I. His son was made king of Numidia by Augustus in B.C. 30.

Orcus: god of the underworld.

Oricus: a port in Epirus.

Orion: a Giant from Boeotia, and a keen hunter, who was killed by Diana for insulting her. He gave his name to a constellation.

Orpheus: husband of Eurydice. Apollo gave him a magic lyre, which could charm gods, men, animals and the whole earth.

Paeligni: a tribe who inhabited a mountainous district in central Italy.

Palatine: one of the Seven Hills of Rome.

Palinurus: a cape in south-west Italy.

Pallas: see Athene.

Parrhasius: a celebrated painter of Ephesus, who flourished about B.C. 400.

Paris: son of Priam (q.v.). His abduction of Helen from Greece caused the Trojan war.

Parthia: an empire situated to the south-east of the Caspian Sea. The Parthians were outstanding as archers, and were perhaps Rome's most feared and hated adversaries.

Patara: a town on the estuary of the river Xanthus (q.v.), where there was an oracle of Apollo.

Paulus, Aemilius: commander with Varro of the Roman army at Cannae (B.C. 216), a famous Carthaginian victory.

Paulus Maximus: consul in B.C. 11 and a friend of Augustus.

Pegasus: a mythological horse, associated with Bellerophon (q.v.).

Peleus: was trapped in a situation similar to that of Bellerophon (q.v.). Hippolyte's husband Acastus left him asleep on Mount Pelion to be devoured by wild beasts, but he survived with the aid of his magic knife.

Pelops: son of Tantalus (q.v.). A curse was laid on him and his descendants (the house of Atreus) as a result of a murder that he committed; for the working out of this curse through the ramifications of his family see under Atreus and Thyestes.

Penelope: wife of Ulysses; a model of virtue.

Phaethon: son of the sun-god. He stole his father's chariot and, unable to control it, was burnt to death.

Phalanthus: a Spartan adventurer who founded Tarentum.

Philippi: a town in Macedonia, where, in B.C. 42, Antony and Octavian defeated Brutus and Cassius. See also under Pollio.

Phraates : a king of Parthia (q.v.) from the Arsacid family. His subjects turned him off the throne, but he regained his position by murdering his substitute.

Phthia : a town in Thessaly.

Pieria : a district on the northern side of Mount Olympus in Thessaly, the home of the Muses.

Pindar : a famous lyric poet, born near Thebes about B.C. 522.

Pirithous : king of the Lapiths (q.v.), who tried to abduct Proserpine from Hades.

Pisa : a town in Elis in the north-west Peloponnese, where the Olympic Games were held.

Plancus, L. Munatius : consul in B.C. 42, when Horace was twenty-three.

Pluto : god of the underworld; he seized and took away Proserpine (q.v.).

Pollio, G. Asinius : held in the highest repute in Horace's day as a writer of tragedies (though none of his works survive), a speaker in the Senate and an advocate. With Maecenas he was a patron of literature, and a friend of both Horace and Virgil. He undertook a history of the Civil Wars, which covered the period from the first consulship of Metellus in B.C. 60, the year when the first triumvirate of Julius Caesar, Crassus and Pompey was formed, down to B.C. 42, the date of the battle of Philippi, where Brutus and Cassius, the leaders of the senatorial party, were killed.

Praeneste : a hill-town near Rome.

Priam : king of Troy at the time of the Trojan war, and father of Hector and Paris.

Proculeius : G. Proculeius Varro divided up his property between his two brothers, who had lost theirs during the Civil Wars.

Proetus : see under Bellerophon.

Prometheus : according to Greek mythology, he made Man from clay, taught him many skills and on his behalf stole fire from heaven. He was punished by Zeus by being chained to a mountain in the Caucasus, where an eagle visited him daily and fed on his liver.

Proserpine : daughter of Ceres (q.v.), and queen of the underworld.

Proteus : a sea-god who tended the flocks of Neptune.

Pyrrha : she and Deucalion, her husband, were the sole survivors of the Flood, according to Roman mythology.

Pyrrhus : king of Epirus, who invaded Italy and had the flower of his army destroyed at Asculum in B.C. 279 (though the victory was nominally his – hence the expression 'a Pyrrhic victory').

Pythagoras : a celebrated Greek philosopher, born about B.C. 580. His best-known theory was that of 'metempsychosis', that is, that when a man dies his soul is reborn later in a new bodily cage, either human or animal. He himself considered that he had been in previous existences in turn a peacock, Euphorbus (a Greek warrior in the Trojan war) and Homer. He proved his point, it is related, by recognising an old shield in Argos as the one he had used at Troy. When the shield was turned, the name of Euphorbus was found on the inside.

Quintilius Varus: a friend of Horace and Virgil, who died in B.C. 24.

Rhode: a girl's name.

Rhodope: a Thracian mountain.

Rhoetus: a Giant (q.v.).

Romulus: legendary first king of Rome.

Sabines: ancient inhabitants of the country just north of Rome; there, at Tibur (q.v.), Horace had his favourite farm.

Salamis: (i) an island near Athens. (ii) a town in Cyprus, founded by Teucer (q.v.).

Salii: 'the jumpers' – the name given to the dancing priests of Mars.

Samos: an island in the Aegean, off the south-west corner of Asia Minor, near where Icarus (q.v.) was drowned.

Sappho: see under Lesbos.

Saturn: father of Jupiter, by whom he was deposed as ruler of heaven.

Scaurus, M. Aemilius: consul in B.C. 115 and 107.

Scipio: P. Scipio Africanus, 'the Elder', led the Roman armies successfully against the Carthaginians, finally crushing Hannibal at the battle of Zama in B.C. 202.

Scopas: a celebrated Parian sculptor, who flourished about B.C. 395–350.

Sestius, Lucius: consul in B.C. 23, who may have fought with Horace under Brutus at Philippi (q.v.).

Simonides: B.C. c. 556–468, a writer of dirges and lyrics, including a famous epigram on the victims of Thermopylae.

Sisyphus: king of Corinth, who for his sins on earth was condemned in Hades to push a large stone up a hill, from which it continually rolled down.

Sithonia: the central peninsula of Chalcidice, in south-east Macedonia.

Soracte: a mountain about 25 miles north of Rome.

Spartacus: leader of the slaves in their rebellion (B.C. 73–71), during which many ravages were committed.

Stesichorus: a Greek poet, who lived about B.C. 600.

Sthenelus: one of the soldiers under Diomede (q.v.).

Styx: one of the rivers of the underworld.

Sygambri: a German tribe; see note to 4.ii.35–36.

Syrtes: the dangerous shoals off the coast of North Africa; also the desert inland.

Tantalus: son of Zeus, father of Pelops and grandfather of Atreus (q.v.). He took advantage of his friendship with the gods by serving them a dish composed of his son's flesh. As a punishment for this he was set hungry and thirsty beside a pool of water, which receded whenever he tried to drink from it.

Tarentum: the modern Taranto, on the 'heel' of Italy.

GLOSSARY

Tarquin: a semi-legendary king of Rome.

Tartarus: the underworld.

Tecmessa: a Trojan princess, whose father was killed by Ajax, son of Telamon (q.v.).

Telegonus: founder of Tusculum in Latium and son of Ulysses, whom he killed by mistake.

Tempe: a valley in Thessaly.

Teos: a town on the west coast of Asia Minor, home of Anacreon.

Teucer: a Greek hero in the Trojan war, half-brother to Ajax, son of Telamon. When he returned home after the war to his home at Salamis, his father banished him, blaming him for Ajax's death.

Thalia: the Muse of comic poetry.

Theseus: a legendary hero and a friend of Pirithous (q.v.). His many exploits included the defeat of the Centaurs at Pirithous' wedding feast: see under Lapiths.

Thurii: a town in southern Italy.

Thyestes: brother of Atreus (q.v.). His own children were served up to him at a banquet given by his brother, on whose house he laid a curse in revenge.

Tibullus: an elegiac poet, contemporary and friend of Horace.

Tibur: a town twenty miles north of Rome, where Horace's favourite farm was.

Tiburnus: the founder of Tibur (q.v.).

Tiridates: became king of Parthia for a short time after the expulsion of Phraates (q.v.), but later lost his throne and sought the protection of Augustus.

Titans: see under Giants.

Tithonus: a mortal loved by Aurora, the dawn goddess, who begged Zeus to grant him eternal life, but omitted to add eternal youth to this request.

Tityos: a Giant who offered outrage to Latona and was killed by Apollo and Diana.

Troilus: son of Priam (q.v.) and Hecuba, killed by Achilles.

Tyrrhene: the sea west of Rome, also called the Tuscan Sea.

Ustica: a valley near Horace's Sabine farm.

Varius, Lucius: a writer of epic poetry, whose verse does not survive.

Vatican: one of the Seven Hills of Rome.

Venafrum: a town in Campania.

Venus (Aphrodite): goddess of love.

Venusia: a town in Apulia (q.v.), where Horace was born.

Virgil: a contemporary poet and friend of Horace, author of the *Aeneid.*

Vulcan: the gods' blacksmith.

Vultur: a mountain near Venusia.

Xanthus: a river that runs through Lycia, in Asia Minor.

MORE ABOUT PENGUINS

Penguinews, which appears every month, contains details of all the new books issued by Penguins as they are published. From time to time it is supplemented by *Penguins in Print*, which is a complete list of all books published by Penguins which are in print. (There are well over four thousand of these.)

A specimen copy of *Penguinews* will be sent to you free on request, and you can become a subscriber for the price of the postage. For a year's issues (including the complete lists) please send 30p if you live in the United Kingdom, or 60p if you live elsewhere. Just write to Dept EP, Penguin Books Ltd, Harmondsworth, Middlesex, enclosing a cheque or postal order, and your name will be added to the mailing list.

Note: *Penguinews* and *Penguins in Print* are not available in the U.S.A. or Canada

THE PENGUIN CLASSICS

Some Recent Volumes

ALESSANDRO MANZONI
The Betrothed *Bruce Penman*

PLATO
Phaedrus and Letters VII and VIII *Walter Hamilton*

ZOLA
The Debacle *Leonard Tancock*

GALDOS
Fortunata and Jacinta *Lester Clark*

BAUDELAIRE
Selected Writings on Art and Artists *Patrick Charvet*

CAMOENS
The Lusiads *W. C. Atkinson*

MONTESQUIEU
Persian Letters *C. J. Betts*

HESIOD and THEOGNIS
Dorothea Wender

NIETZSCHE
Beyond Good and Evil *R. J. Hollingdale*

PLUTARCH
The Age of Alexander *Ian Scott Kilvert*

WU CH'ENG-EN
Monkey *Arthur Waley*